Anglais

New Live

5e

Odile Plays Martin-Cocher
Collège Rives du Léman, Évian
Académie de Grenoble

Danielle Serpollet
Agrégée de l'université

Avec la collaboration de
Anne Grzesiak-Lycett
B.A. Honours (Hull)
DESS de formateur en langues

Workbook

Didier
13, rue de l'Odéon - 75006 Paris

Message aux élèves...

Bienvenue en 5e !
Te voilà de nouveau dans les *"starting blocks"*, au début d'une nouvelle année d'anglais.
Voici quelques conseils pour ton travail à la maison : prends le temps de les lire !

• Avant de faire les exercices donnés par ton professeur, relis attentivement tout ce qui a été fait en cours : les notes prises dans le cahier d'anglais, le dialogue ou le texte de la leçon, la partie grammaticale *And now think!*

• Dans ton *workbook*, fais les exercices au crayon à papier, pour pouvoir gommer et corriger proprement et lisiblement.

Il est important que tes corrections soient très claires : tu en auras besoin pour réviser avant un devoir en classe.

• Ne bâcle pas les exercices : si ce que tu écris est faux, tu risques de mémoriser des erreurs.

Travaille dans le calme et la concentration.

• Après avoir fait tes devoirs, vérifie en deux ou trois minutes si tu sais ta leçon.

Imagine-toi en cours d'anglais : tu prends la parole pour raconter l'histoire, poser des questions ou répondre aux questions de tes camarades, jouer un dialogue, etc. Si tu y parviens mentalement sans hésitation, cela prouve que tu sais ta leçon !

Enfin, souviens-toi qu'apprendre une langue étrangère exige beaucoup de régularité dans le travail personnel. C'est la clé de la réussite !

Bonne année scolaire !

Conseil pratique :
Fabrique-toi deux caches, un pour le livre et un pour le *workbook*. Procure-toi une feuille cartonnée de format A4. Coupe-la en deux dans le sens de la longueur. Écris ton nom sur chaque cache. Tu pourras t'en servir pour cacher les textes enregistrés pendant le cours, mais aussi comme marque-page !

Ce *workbook* appartient à : .... Classe de : ....

ISBN 2 - 278 - 05053 - 2

Imprimé en France

b) Note les répliques correspondantes extraites de la B.D. page 15 de ton livre.

Pour demander une permission : ....

Pour demander à qui appartient quelque chose : ....

Pour demander ce que quelqu'un fait : ....

Pour demander qui est absent : ....

Pour dire bonjour : ....

Pour dire à qui appartient quelque chose : ....

Pour dire ce qu'on fait : ....

Pour dire ce que quelqu'un a (ce qui ne va pas) : ....

Pour saluer en partant : ....

Pour s'excuser d'être en retard : ....

UNIT 1

LESSON 1

2 Listen and speak

- Le texte enregistré reproduit ici doit être caché pendant l'exercice d'écoute.
- Il te servira de modèle, au besoin, pendant l'activité orale.
- Tu pourras en mémoriser quelques phrases avant un contrôle oral ou écrit.

Jim: Find my cousin on this photo.
Mary: Is it a girl?
Jim: Yes, it is.
Mary: Is she tall?
Jim: No, she isn't.
Mary: Has she got dark hair?
Jim: Yes, she has.
Mary: Has she got short dark hair?
Jim: No, she hasn't.
Mary: Has she got green eyes?
Jim: Yes, she has.
Mary: So. It's a girl, she's small, she has got dark hair...
Jim: Yes, long dark hair and green eyes.
Mary: Is she nice?
Jim: Yes, she is!

3 Listen and understand

a) Regarde les images et décris-les.

Picture 1. *You:* Tracy has got short brown hair. She's in ...

b) Écoute et dis tout ce que tu as compris.

c) Écoute à nouveau en regardant les illustrations ci-dessous et ajoute des informations sur les héros.

d) Récapitule tout ce que tu sais sur chaque personnage.

You: Tracy has got a brother. She ...

MEMO

NEW WORDS

- hair - eye - nose - a show-off - a mess
- bright = intelligent - short ≠ long - tall ≠ small - dark ≠ fair - great fun - top of the class

AND NOW... THINK!

1. a) Observe ces trois phrases concernant Melissa, qui comportent la contraction *'s*. Écris les formes pleines en dessous. Assure-toi que tu sais conjuguer *Be* et *have got* au présent (voir tableaux de conjugaison page 137).

She's very bright. She's got lots of books. She's top of the class.

....

b) *Have got* s'emploie pour exprimer ce que quelqu'un possède (y compris ses caractéristiques physiques). Trouve deux exemples dans la leçon :

....

....

2. *Is he nice? - Has she got long hair? - Is he a show-off?*

Comment se construit la forme interrogative ?

....

Invente des réponses à ces questions.

....

Comment appelle-t-on ces réponses ? ....

Pour les construire, on garde : ....

On ne répète pas : ....

3. Lis les deux phrases suivantes et souligne les noms en bleu et les adjectifs épithètes en rouge.

I've got blond hair and green eyes. He's got big blue eyes.

En anglais, les adjectifs épithètes se placent généralement .... le nom qu'ils qualifient.

Attention ! En français : c'est pareil ❑, c'est le contraire ❑.

at home

memorize

❶ Complète les phrases suivantes puis vérifie dans le texte encadré page 3 ci-dessus.

Mary: Is she tall?

Jim: No, ...

Mary: Has she got dark hair?

Jim: Yes, ...

Mary: Has she got short dark hair?

Jim: No, ...

Mary: .... green eyes?

Jim: Yes, she has.

Mary: .... nice?

Jim: Yes, she is!

read

❷ Chaque description de personnage comprend trois erreurs. Retrouve-les et corrige-les de mémoire ou en relisant les textes page 19 de ton livre.

- Hello! I'm Tracy Charlton. I'm 12 and I've got blond hair and blue eyes.
- This is my little sister: tall with a funny nose. She's okay.
- This is Tracy Charlton, she's my best friend. She's great fun.

....

- Hi, my name's Robin Charlton. I'm 13, intelligent, funny-looking and I've got big blue eyes.
- Robin, my big brother, he's a show-off and his room is always tidy.
- Ah! This is Robin Charlton. He's a clown but he is very mean.

....

- I'm Melissa Roberts. I'm 13, I've got two little sisters and a baby brother. I'm in Tracy's class.
- This is Melissa Roberts. She's very bright! She's top of the class!
- This is my best friend. Her poems are great and she's got lots of toys in her room.

....

practise

3 Complète les phrases suivantes avec l'auxiliaire *Be* ou *Have* correctement conjugué.

The Charltons

Mr Charlton .... a very nice man. He .... tall and he .... got short brown hair. His eyes .... brown. His wife, Mrs Charlton, ... small and very pretty. She .... got short brown hair and blue eyes. They .... got two children and they .... very good parents!

4 Imagine les questions correspondant aux réponses suivantes :

1. ....
– Yes, she is. (she = Melissa)

2. ....
– No, he hasn't. (he = Robin)

3. ....
– Yes, she has. (she = Tracy)

4. ....
– Yes, she has. (she = Melissa)

5. ....
– Yes, he is. (he = Robin)

write

5 Rédige une courte présentation de toi-même et entraîne-toi à te présenter comme si tu étais devant tes camarades.

....

....

....

....

....

....

....

LESSON 2

2 Listen and speak

a) Écoute et complète ce tableau.

	♥	✗♥	☀♥	so-so	Why or why not?
Myriam					
music					....
maths					....
Mark					
science					....
English					....
Tim					
art					....
geography					....

Help: fun
cool
interesting ≠ boring
easy ≠ hard = difficult

easy

difficult

boring

- Le texte enregistré reproduit ici doit être caché pendant l'exercice d'écoute.
- Il te servira de modèle, au besoin, pendant l'activité orale.
- Tu pourras en mémoriser quelques phrases avant un contrôle oral ou écrit.

Tim: Myriam, do you like music?
Myriam: Yes, I do, it's fun.
Tim: What about maths?
Myriam: I hate it, it's boring.
Tim: Does Mark like science?
Myriam: Yes, he does, he thinks it's interesting.
Tim: Does he like English too?
Myriam: Oh yes, he loves it, he says it's cool.
Tim, do you like art?
Tim: Yes, I like it a lot, it's easy.
Myriam: What about geography?
Tim: So-so, it's really hard.

3 Read and understand

a) Lis les textes page 21 de ton livre et retrouve les prénoms puis complète les informations manquantes.

NAMES	SPORTS	MUSIC	BOOKS AND FILMS
1.	♡ gymnastics	☼♡ music but doesn't play an	
2.	☼♡ .... ✗♡ hiking		♡ watching videos and DVDs
3.		♡	
4.	♡ .... climbing		
5.	♡ horse-riding ✗♡ swimming		♡ ....
6.	✗♡	not	☼♡ science fiction and mystery books

b) Et toi ? Parle des activités que tu aimes faire... ou non !

MEMO

NEW WORDS

- easy ≠ difficult, hard - interesting ≠ boring - cool - musical
- hiking - horse-riding - climbing
- mystery - comics

love
enjoy / like a lot
like
don't like very much
don't like at all
hate

AND NOW... THINK!

1. ***Kate likes gymnastics.***

Cette phrase permet :

❑ de décrire l'activité de Kate,

❑ de caractériser Kate.

Cette phrase est au présent parce que :

❑ Kate aime la gymnastique uniquement au moment où je le dis,

❑ Kate aime la gymnastique tout le temps, donc aussi au moment où j'en parle.

• Ce présent est appelé "présent simple". Souligne le verbe dans l'exemple. Pourquoi ce temps est-il simple ?

....

• Quel auxiliaire va-t-on utiliser pour construire les formes négative et interrogative ?

....

Trouve deux exemples :

....

....

Attention : Une seule marque du temps par phrase ! Quand l'auxiliaire est là, c'est lui qui est conjugué. Ex. : *He doesn't like sports.*

2. (1) ***She loves music.***

(2) ***He doesn't like hiking.***

(3) ***She enjoys riding her bike.***

Les verbes de goût peuvent être suivis d'un .... comme en (1) ou d'un nom verbal comme en (2) et (3), que l'on forme ainsi :

.... + ...

at home

memorize

❶ Regarde ton emploi du temps et écris en anglais le nom des disciplines que tu étudies cette année puis vérifie dans ton livre page 20.

....

....

....

2 Relis le texte encadré page 7 ci-dessus puis, sans le regarder, complète les dialogues. Vérifie ensuite.

Tim: Myriam, ... you .... music?

Myriam: Yes, I do, it's f....................................

Tim: What about maths?

Myriam: I hate it, it's b....................................

Tim: .... Mark like science?

Myriam: Yes, he ...., he thinks it's i....................................

Tim: Does he like English too?

Myriam: Oh yes, he loves it, he says it's c....................................

Tim, do you like art?

Tim: Yes, I like it ...., it's e....................................

Myriam: What about geography?

Tim: So- ...., it's really h....................................

read

3 Peux-tu compléter les textes ci-dessous ? Remets les mots suivants à leur place puis vérifie à la page 21 de ton livre.

playing - music - swimming - play - hiking - riding - reading - canoeing - watching - sport

Kate:
She likes gymnastics. She loves .... but she doesn't .... an instrument.

Andrew:
He likes music a lot and he enjoys .... the trumpet.

Tim:
He doesn't like .... and he is no good at it. He isn't musical. He loves science fiction and mystery books.

Kevin:
He loves sports. He likes .... his bike, hiking and climbing.

Sean:
He loves ...., but he doesn't like .... at all.

He enjoys .... videos and DVDs.

Isabel:
She enjoys horse-riding but she doesn't like .... very much.

She likes .... comics.

practise

4 **a) À partir de la grille suivante, écris trois petits textes décrivant les goûts de John, Fiona et Derek :**

Names	English	Geography	Physical Education
John			
Fiona			
Derek			

John hates

Fiona

Derek

b) Rédige trois phrases, une pour chacun, qui explique un de leurs goûts... ou dégoûts. À toi d'imaginer leurs raisons.

write

5 **Écris trois phrases pour dire ce que tu aimes faire quand tu n'es pas en classe. Utilise chaque fois un verbe différent.**

LESSON 3

2 Listen and speak

- Le texte enregistré reproduit ici doit être caché pendant l'exercice d'écoute.
- Il te servira de modèle, au besoin, pendant l'activité orale.
- Tu pourras en mémoriser quelques phrases avant un contrôle oral ou écrit.

Bob is going to visit his aunt in Linton.
Bob: Er... tell me, Auntie, is there a swimming pool in Linton?
Auntie Flo: Yes, there's one opposite the school.
Bob: Great! Is there a baseball field too?
Auntie Flo: Oh no, there isn't, but there's a theatre!
Bob: Oh! Where is it?
Auntie Flo: Next to the school.
Bob: Ah! And... are there any cinemas?
Auntie Flo: No, there aren't, but there's a big toy store opposite the theatre.
Bob: A toy store! Auntie! I'm 14... I'm not a baby any more!

c) Now, speak!

1. Invente ton centre commercial. Complète ton plan à l'aide de la liste ci-dessous. Entoure ce que tu as choisi :

1 shoe shop	1 toy store	1 pub	1 or 2 music store(s)
1 newsagent's	1 pharmacy	1 or 2 restaurant(s)	

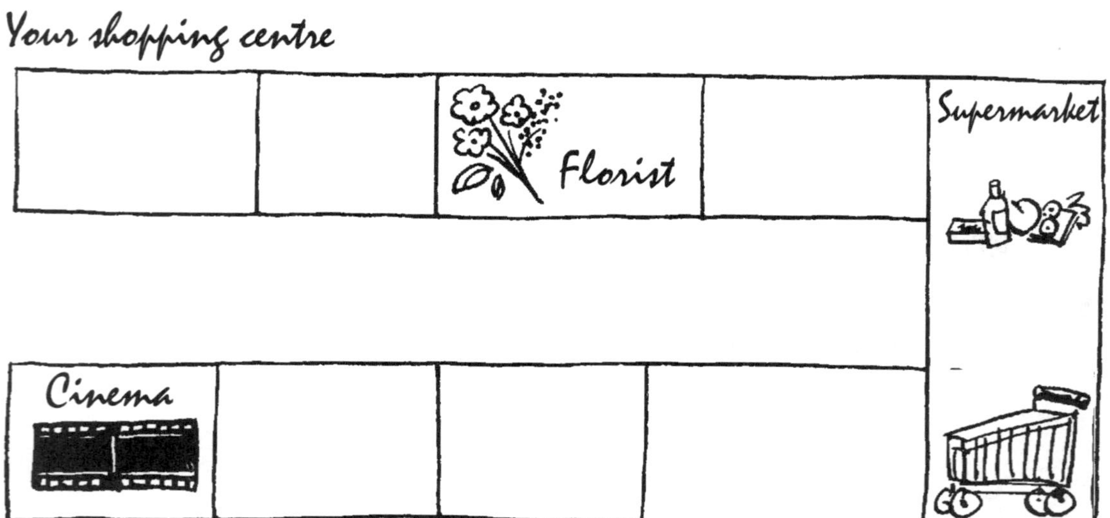

2. Interroge ton ami(e) et coche dans la liste les commerces qu'il/elle a choisis. Attention : quand il peut y en avoir deux, pose la question au pluriel !

You: Is there a ... in your shopping centre?
Your friend: Yes, there's one./No, there isn't.
You: Are there any ...s?
Your friend: Yes, there are 2./No, there aren't (any).

- ❑ 1 shoe shop
- ❑ 1 newsagent's
- ❑ 1 toy store
- ❑ 1 pharmacy
- ❑ 1 pub
- ❑ 1 or ❑ 2 restaurant(s)
- ❑ 1 or ❑ 2 music store(s)

3. Maintenant, tu vas devoir trouver comment ton ami(e) a disposé ses commerces. Pose-lui des questions en te servant de la liste que tu as cochée ci-dessus et note ses réponses sur le plan ci-dessous :

You: Where's your restaurant?
Your friend: It's next to ...

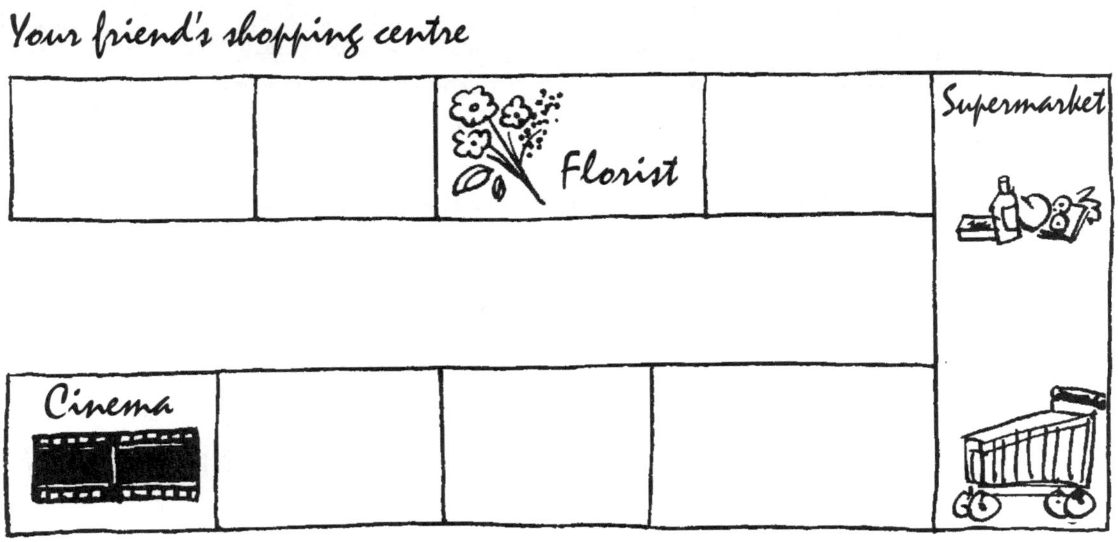

3 Listen and understand

a) Regarde le plan de l'école et décris-le en détail.

You: The Gym is next to ...

b) Ferme ton livre. Maintenant regarde le plan ci-dessous : il est incomplet. Écoute les explications du principal et complète-le.

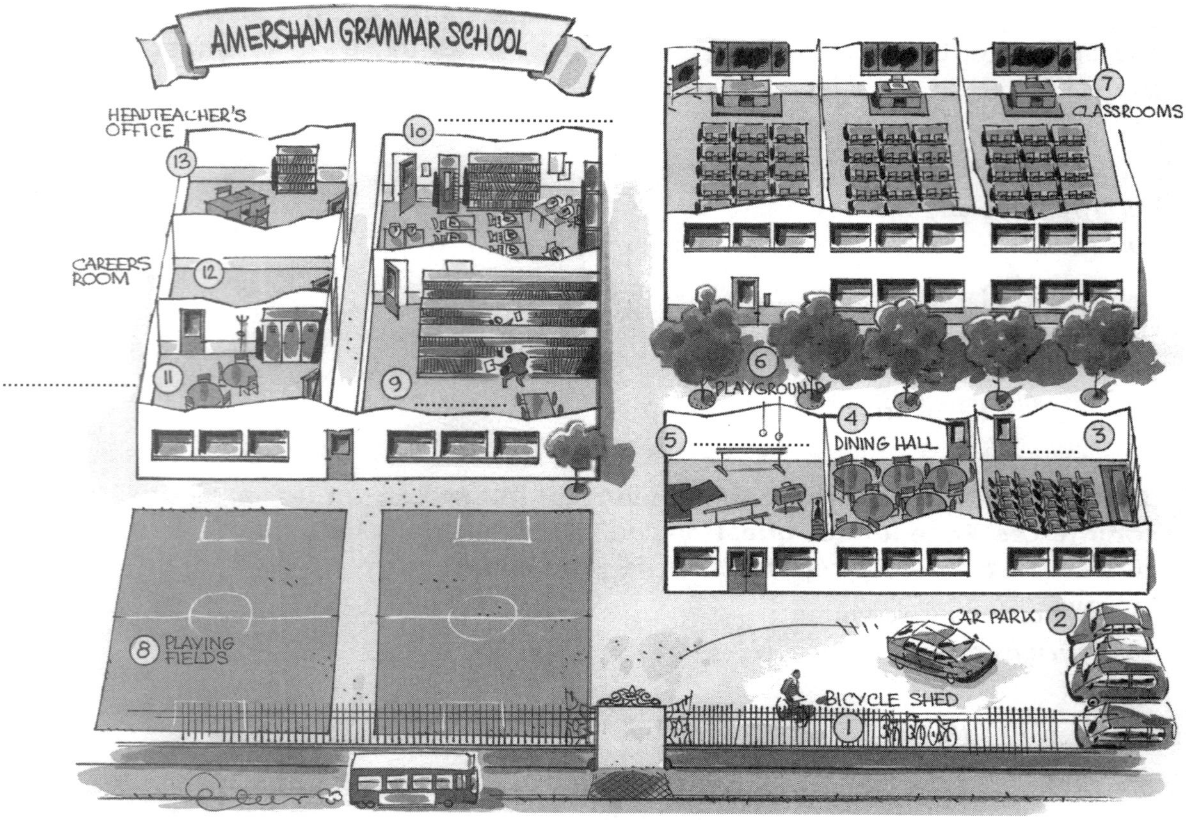

c) **Ce panneau d'informations sur Amersham school est incomplet. Lis-le puis écoute à nouveau pour le compléter.**

AMERSHAM GRAMMAR SCHOOL
.... : *Mr Attley*
New .... teacher: *Miss Parker*
Number of teachers: ....
Number of pupils: ....
Number of classrooms: ....
School orchestra? ❑ *Yes* ❑ *No*
Number of clubs: ....

d) **Vérifie tes notes auprès de tes camarades. Tu résumeras ensuite tout ce que tu sais sur Amersham Grammar School.**

Pupil 1: Who's Mr Attley?
Pupil 2: He's the ...
Pupil 3: How many teachers are there?
Pupil 4: There are ...

e) Compare l'école de nos héros et ton collège. Pour cela relie les colonnes avec des stylos de couleur différente pour chaque école.

Pupil 1: In my school there isn't an orchestra.
Pupil 2: In our school there are some playing fields too.

		• playing fields
there is •	• a/an •	• gym
there are •	• some •	• I.T. room
there isn't •	• 2, 3, 4, ... •	• library
there aren't •	• lots of •	• orchestra
	• any •	• clubs
		• careers room

MEMO

NEW WORDS • headteacher - hall - library - staff room - playing field - office - dining hall - playground - toy store - station - shoe shop

on the left on the right

in front of

next to

across

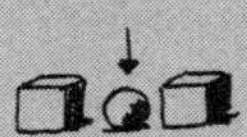

between

opposite

AND NOW... THINK!

1. Traduis ces deux phrases en français.

There is a school orchestra.

....

There are lots of different clubs.

....

Quelles différences y a-t-il entre le français et l'anglais ?

a) En anglais, on utilise le verbe .... alors qu'en français, on utilise le verbe ....

b) En anglais, le verbe s'accorde alors qu'en français, il est ....

2. Observe ces exemples et complète les phrases suivantes avec *some* ou *any* :

There are some very big trees.
Are there any questions?
There aren't any cinemas.

- On emploie .... quand on s'interroge sur l'existence de quelque chose.
- On emploie .... quand on est sûr de l'existence de quelque chose.
- On emploie *not* + ... quand on sait que quelque chose n'existe pas.

Relis les trois phrases ci-dessus et réfléchis : tu as des bonbons et tu en proposes à un(e) ami(e). Que dis-tu ? Complète avec *some* ou *any* :

Do you want .... sweets?

- On emploie .... car on ne s'interroge pas sur l'existence des bonbons mais sur le fait de savoir si l'ami(e) en veut ou pas.

3. Observe l'exemple et complète la phrase suivante :

How many clubs are there? There are three.

"How many" permet d'interroger sur le ....

Le nom qui le suit est toujours au ....

Remarque : La question est toujours au pluriel :

How many restaurants are there? There is one.

at home

memorize

1 Remets à leur place les expressions suivantes : *there's (2) - Is there (2) - there isn't - are there - there aren't,* puis vérifie dans le texte encadré page 12 ci-dessus.

Bob: Er... tell me, auntie, ... a swimming pool in Linton?

Auntie Flo: Yes, ... one opposite the school.

Bob: Great! .... a baseball field too?

Auntie Flo: Oh no, ..., but there's a theatre!

Bob: Oh! Where is it?

Auntie Flo: Next to the school.

Bob: Ah! And... .... any cinemas?

Auntie Flo: No, ... but .... a big toy store opposite the theatre.

Bob: A toy store! Auntie! I'm 14... I'm not a baby any more!

read

2 Lis le dialogue page 23 de ton livre et corrige les affirmations suivantes :

1. There are twenty-eight teachers and five hundred and forty-two pupils.

....

2. The library is opposite the IT room.

....

3. There isn't a school orchestra.

....

4. They've got three new playing fields this year.

....

5. Mr Attley's office is opposite the staff room.

....

practise

3 Complète les phrases suivantes avec : *is* ou *are*, *a* ou *any*.

1. .... there .... library in your school?
2. There .... two cinemas opposite the station.
3. There .... an orchestra and lots of clubs.
4. .... there .... playing fields?
5. There .... music room too.

4 Traduis les phrases suivantes :

1. Il y a 32 professeurs dans mon école.

....

2. Y a-t-il un marchand de journaux dans ce centre commercial ?

....

3. Est-ce qu'il y a des clubs dans une école française ?

....

write

5 Tu écris à ton correspondant et lui décris ce qu'il y a comme magasins et lieux de loisirs (cinéma, terrain de sports, piscine, etc.) dans ton quartier.

In my neighbourhood, there ....

....

....

RHYTHM'N SOUNDS

1. Écoute ces mots puis écris-les dans la colonne correspondant au son entendu.

fine - hey! - how - fair - bright - nice - clown - eyes - now - write
hair - baby - play - great - brown - away - where - bye - Tracy - wear.

[aɪ]	[eɪ]	[aʊ]	[eə]
fine -	*hey!* -	*how* -	*fair* - ....
.... -	.... -	.... -	.... - ....
.... -	.... -		

2. La lettre "o" correspond à plusieurs sons en anglais. Lis les quatre mots qui suivent et écoute comment ils se prononcent.

[ʌ] come	[əʊ] go	[ɒ] golf	[uː] school
.... -	.... -	.... -	.... - ....
.... -	.... -	.... -	.... - ....

Tu vas maintenant entendre une série de mots comportant la lettre "o", inscris chaque mot dans la bonne colonne, c'est-à-dire sous le mot dont le "o" se prononce de la même manière. Voici la série de mots :

home - Robin - do - love - grow - off - open - food - hot - too - not - room - money

STRATEGIES

B • Lis les phrases 1 à 6. Surligne tous les mots que tu connais ou reconnais. Puis prends un crayon de couleur différente et souligne les mots qui sont répétés plusieurs fois.

1 NEVER go away with a stranger

2 NEVER get into a stranger's car

3 NEVER accept sweets or money from a stranger

4 ALWAYS play with friends - never alone

5 ALWAYS be back home before dark

6 ALWAYS tell your mum or dad where you are going and when you will be back

7 If you are ever frightened, ask an adult lady for help - or go to a police officer

C • 1. Si tu ne connais pas le sens du mot *"stranger"*, réponds aux questions suivantes :

Est-ce : ❑ un nom ? ❑ un adjectif ? ❑ un verbe ?

Qu'est-ce qui peut m'aider à comprendre ce mot ?

❑ le dessin
❑ la disposition du texte
❑ la ressemblance avec le français
❑ ce qui est écrit avant
❑ ce qui est écrit après

Donne ta traduction de *"stranger"* : ❑ étrange ❑ étranger ❑ chauffeur

2. Si tu ne connais pas le sens du mot *"rules"* utilisé dans le titre, suis la même démarche :

C'est un ....

Ce qui m'a aidé :

Ma traduction de *"rules"* : ❑ mode d'emploi ❑ proverbes ❑ règles (règlement)

3. Relis la phrase 4. Si tu ne connais pas le sens du mot *"alone"*, sers-toi de ton sens logique :

La règle 4 est constituée de deux phrases : *Always play with friends - Never alone.*

À ton avis ces deux phrases disent :

❑ deux choses complètement différentes ❑ la même chose autrement.

Tu sais que "*always*" et "*never*" sont :

❑ synonymes ❑ contraires

Donc "*play with your friends*" et "*play alone*" sont :

❑ synonymes ❑ contraires

Donne ta traduction de "*alone*" :

Joue toujours avec des amis - jamais... ❑ avec un voisin ❑ avec un adulte ❑ seul

4. Dans la phrase 7, tu ne connais pas le mot *"frightened"* et seul ce qui est dit après peut t'aider. Sachant que *"If you ... ever..."* signifie *"Si jamais tu..."*, peux-tu dire, en relisant la suite de la phrase, si *"frightened"* a un sens positif ou négatif ? Essaie de proposer une traduction puis vérifie dans un dictionnaire.

....

D • Regarde bien les sept illustrations à la page 27 de ton livre. Note ci-dessous la règle qui correspond à chaque illustration :

a) ....

b) ....

c) ....

d) ....

e) ....

f) ....

g) ....

HIGHLIGHTS

1. School Assembly. Read the text and take notes in the grid.

Where?	When?	Who?	Why?

2. School uniforms. Read the text and find the names of the clothes.

3. Sports day. Is it true or false? If it's false, correct the sentence.

- Sports day is usually at the beginning of the school year. ....
- The pupils compete for their forms. ....
- It is a very important event. ....

• **There are usually four houses in a British school. Imagine names for the four houses.** ....

4. Malton School.

• **The students organised a sponsored walk and raised money: now they have new** .... **and** ....

• **Some students went on short trips. What for? Find three reasons.**

To ....

....

• **They had a non-uniform day. Who did they help?** ....

How much did they raise? ....

• **When do you get a commendation?** ....

....

LEARN YOUR WORDS

1. **Complète la liste des mots qui décrivent le corps humain avec tous les mots que tu connais. Enrichis ton vocabulaire en allant rechercher dans le lexique pages 145-164 les mots que tu ne connais pas.**

2. **Remplis la grille avec les mots suivants, puis trouves-en trois de plus pour chaque catégorie. Enrichis ton vocabulaire à l'aide du lexique.**

tourist information
trainers
street
station
dress
cheese
coffee
jelly
cake
socks
orange juice
water
coke
chocolate
music store
sweatshirt

clothes & shoes	food & drinks	the city

MAINTENANT TU SAIS

Lesson 1
- Dire ce que quelqu'un possède — *She has got lots of books.*
- Décrire quelqu'un et dire son âge — *He has got blue eyes. He's 13.*
- Interroger et répondre — *Has he got blond hair? Yes, he has./No, he hasn't.*

Lesson 2
- Parler des goûts — *She likes music. I love Art. We enjoy swimming.*
- Interroger sur les goûts de quelqu'un — *Do you like sports?*
- Répondre — *Yes, I do./No, I don't.*

Lesson 3
- Dire que quelque chose existe, ou non — *There is a gym next to the dining hall. There are some big trees. There aren't any clubs.*
- Interroger sur l'existence — *Are there any restaurants?*
- Interroger sur le nombre — *How many clubs are there?*

Strategies
- Repérer le type de document avant de lire, s'appuyer sur le connu, sur les mots transparents et sur les redondances pour en tirer du sens, deviner le sens de mots inconnus.

UNIT 2

LESSON 1

at school

2 Listen and speak

- Le texte enregistré reproduit ici doit être caché pendant l'exercice d'écoute.
- Il te servira de modèle, au besoin, pendant l'activité orale.
- Tu pourras en mémoriser quelques phrases avant un contrôle oral ou écrit.

1. They live in Australia. What do they eat? Leaves. They carry their babies in their pouches and on their backs. What do they do during the day? They sleep.
2. They live in Alaska. What colour are they? They are grey and they eat fish. Where do they sleep? In the snow.
3. Where do they live? In North America, in the woods. They eat nuts, berries, leaves and insects. What do they do all day? They climb up and down trees. Where do they sleep? In nests.

3 Listen and understand

a) Look at the comic strip and make a list of words you expect to hear. You can ask for help.

You: How do you say *"reptile"* in English?
Teacher: Reptile!

....

....

....

b) Listen and tick the words you hear in your list.

c) Listen again and write down more words.

....

....

d) Listen again and check, then recap what you know about Komodo dragons. Use your lists of words.

e) "Life's great for dragons!": Why?
"They're dangerous": Why?

MEMO

NEW WORDS

- forest - wood - tree - branch(es) - leaf (leaves)
- Food: grass - nut(s) - berry (berries) - insect(s) - meat
- live - happen - sleep - kill - eat - drink
- dead - hungry - strong
- during - only

look at

look for

look like

AND NOW... THINK!

1. ***This is Varri! It looks like a prehistoric monster.***

Dragons just eat and sleep and sleep and eat!

They eat meat. They don't eat fruit.

a) Lis les exemples et coche la bonne case :

❑ Les informations relevées sont vraies uniquement au moment où Robin parle.

❑ Les informations relevées sont vraies quel que soit le moment où on les donne.

b) Quel est le temps employé ? ....

Ce temps sert ici à exprimer des caractéristiques du sujet grammatical (les dragons).

2. Quand je dis : ***Beavers build their houses,***

❑ Je parle de quelques castors en particulier.

❑ Je généralise : je parle de l'ensemble des castors.

Attention : Comment traduirais-tu cette phrase en français ?

....

Quelle remarque fais-tu ?

....

memorize

1 Replace les questions au bon endroit et vérifie ensuite dans le texte encadré page 22 ci-dessus.

What do they eat? - Where do they live? - What do they do during the day? - Where do they sleep? (2) - What colour are they?

1. They live in Australia. ....? Leaves. They carry their babies in their pouches and on their backs. ....? They sleep.

2. They live in Alaska. ....? They are grey and they eat fish. ....? In the snow.

3. ....? In North America, in the woods. They eat nuts, berries, leaves and insects. What do they do all day? They climb up and down trees. ....? In nests.

read

2 Corrige les sept erreurs qui se sont glissées dans ces phrases sur les dragons de Komodo et vérifie ensuite dans ton livre page 33.

a) They just eat and play and play and eat.

....

b) They get up early and go and look for dinner.

....

c) They're omnivorous and dangerous.

....

d) Look at this one! It's very strong. When it's thirsty, it kills an enormous animal and eats it up in twenty minutes.

....

practise

3 a) Tu vas t'occuper de trois lapins ce week-end. Lis la fiche et récapitule par écrit.

THE 3 RABBITS:

(Yes): They eat .... and ....

(No): They ....

They .... milk.

(?): .... they ....?

b) Tu vas t'occuper d'une petite chatte ce week-end. Lis la fiche et récapitule par écrit.

MILLIE THE CAT:

(Yes): She .... and ....

She .... milk.

(No): She ....

(?): .... she ....?

4 Complète cette interview :

Robin: Where .... you ....?

Baloo: In the jungle.

Robin: .... all day?

Baloo: I .... food, then I play with my ....

Robin: ....?

Baloo: Yes, and fruit too.

Robin: .... sleep?

Baloo: At night, of course!

write

platypus

5 Pose cinq questions à propos de l'ornithorynque.

....

....

....

....

....

LESSON 2

2 Listen and speak

a) Listen to Mr Attley's questions and match the three columns.

	• never •	
Kelly •	• not very often •	• 
Mark •	• sometimes •	• 
Thomas •	• often •	• 
	• always •	

- Le texte enregistré reproduit ici doit être caché pendant l'exercice d'écoute.
- Il te servira de modèle, au besoin, pendant l'activité orale.
- Tu pourras en mémoriser quelques phrases avant un contrôle oral ou écrit.

1. *Mr Attley:* Kelly, do you always listen in class?
Kelly: Yes, I always do.
Mr Attley: Always?
Kelly: Yes, always.

2. *Mr Attley:* Mark, do you sometimes chat in class?
Mark: No, I don't.
Mr Attley: Really?
Mark: Er... well... not very often.

3. *Mr Attley:* Thomas, do you often do your homework in front of the television?
Thomas: No, never!
Mr Attley: Oh, really?
Thomas: Er... well... sometimes.

3 Listen and understand

a) Look at the pictures then imagine what sort of pupil Melissa is and what she likes.

Class: She always ... / sometimes ...
She loves ...

b) Listen and check your predictions.

Class: She doesn't always ..., but she ...

c) Listen again and recap.

Class: Melissa often ... because she loves ...
She doesn't ... because ...

d) What sort of pupil are you? Read the quiz and draw a circle round your answers, tot up your hearts, diamonds, clubs and spades (♥, ♦, ♣ and ♠) then read your results!

Do you often ...?	never	sometimes	often	always
1 ... forget a book or an exercise book?	♥	♦	♣	♠
2 ... ask questions in class?	♠	♣	♦	♥
3 ... do your homework in front of the television?	♥	♦	♣	♠
4 ... help a friend with his/her homework?	♠	♣	♦	♥
5 ... chat during lessons?	♥	♦	♣	♠
6 ... eat chewing-gum during lessons?	♥	♦	♣	♠
7 ... sleep in class?	♥	♦	♣	♠

♥ = 4 ♦ = 3 ♣ = 2 ♠ = 1	
28 - 22	You are the perfect pupil. You always do exactly what is right! Congratulations!
21 - 14	You try hard to be a good pupil. Keep up the good work!
13 - 8	Do you sometimes get bad marks? Are you often in detention? Pull your socks up!
7 - 1	School is hell for you... and for your teachers! Remember: Punishments are extra homework, so think twice!

MEMO

NEW WORDS

- chat - forget - surf - work - help someone with...
- computer - homework
- never sometimes often always
- Sure! - Go ahead! - In fact

AND NOW... THINK!

1. Lis ces phrases :

He never forgets his homework.
Do you always listen in class?
She sometimes chats in class.

Elles comportent toutes des adverbes de fréquence. Observe la place de ces adverbes et coche la bonne réponse.

Les adverbes de fréquence tels que : *sometimes, always, often, never* se placent en général immédiatement : avant ❑ après ❑ le verbe qu'ils modifient.

2. a) Dans les phrases suivantes, souligne en rouge le verbe conjugué et en bleu les compléments.

I like working in my room with my cat and my music.
I enjoy working with him.
She loves surfing the Internet.

Combien y a-t-il de verbes conjugués par phrase? ....

b) Observe ces phrases et traduis-les.

I like music. - I like sports.

....

I like swimming. - I like running.

....

Pourquoi *"swimming"* et *"running"* sont-ils appelés des noms verbaux dans ces phrases ?

....

c) Complète la règle :

Après des verbes exprimant les goûts, comme par exemple ...., ..., et ...., on peut trouver des noms ou des .... (B.V.+*ing*).

at home

memorize

1 **Réécris les questions en ajoutant l'adverbe de fréquence puis vérifie dans le texte encadré page 26 ci-dessus.**

Interview 1:
- Kelly, do you listen in class?
- .... *(always)*

Interview 2:
- Mark, do you chat in class?
- .... *(sometimes)*

Interview 3:
- Thomas, do you do your homework in front of the television?
- .... *(often)*

read

2 **Corrige les six erreurs qui se sont glissées dans le résumé de l'interview de Melissa.**

Melissa never chats with her friend Nora. She sometimes does her homework.

....

She enjoys working in her room with her dog and her music. She often asks

....

questions in her art class because she hates surfing the Internet. Melissa always helps

....

Tracy with her homework because Tracy enjoys doing her homework.

....

practise

3 **Lis les phrases suivantes et déduis-en les goûts des personnages.**

Exemple : Bob runs every morning: *he enjoys running.*

1. Kevin always forgets his tennis racket: *he hates* ....
2. Melissa paints every weekend: *she loves* ....
3. Mrs Charlton is not a very good cook: ....
4. Robin plays cricket every Saturday: ....
5. Tracy often goes to the swimming pool: ....

....

write

4 **Tu fais partie du comité de rédaction du journal de ton collège et tu es chargé(e) de rédiger le questionnaire :** ***What sort of friend are you?*** **Écris cinq questions. Voici quelques verbes qui peuvent t'aider.**

Help! phone - play - go - send: *envoyer* - quarrel: *se disputer*

1. Do you often ....?
2. ....
3. ....
4. ....
5. ....

LESSON 3

at school

2 Listen and speak

- Le texte enregistré reproduit ici doit être caché pendant l'exercice d'écoute.
- Il te servira de modèle, au besoin, pendant l'activité orale.
- Tu pourras en mémoriser quelques phrases avant un contrôle oral ou écrit.

1. *Nelly:* Pam, what about going to the cinema?
Pam: Oh no, Nelly, I don't want to sit and watch a movie.
Nelly: Why don't we go to the swimming pool?
Pam: I don't want to go to the pool. It's too late!
Nelly: What do you want to do, then?
Pam: I want to try my new bike.
Nelly: Okay, let's go then!

2. *Greg:* Alison, what about watching television?
Alison: Greg, please! I don't want to sit and watch a movie.
Greg: Why don't we go to the swimming pool?
Alison: I don't want to go to the pool. It's too cold!
Greg: What do you want to do, then?
Alison: I want to try my new rollerblades.
Greg: Okay, let's go then!

3. *Peter:* Keith, what about watching sport on television?
Keith: Peter, please! I don't want to sit and watch a stupid game.
Peter: Why don't we read comics?
Keith: Oh no! Let's go to the park!
Peter: But... What do you want to do in the park?
Keith: I want to try my new kite.
Peter: Okay, let's go then!

3 Listen and understand

a) Listen to the beginning of the dialogue. What does Tracy want to do? What about Melissa?

Class: Tracy wants to ...
Melissa wants to ... . She doesn't want to ...

b) Look at the pictures p. 37. What do the kids do in these different clubs?

Class: In the nature club, they ...

In the astronomy club, they ...

c) Listen and find the club the two girls want to start.

d) Now, recap.

Class: Tracy ... a new club, but Melissa doesn't want to ... . She wants to ...
Tracy wants to ..., but Melissa says there are ...
Then they decide to ...

e) Explain what a "get-together" club is.

Class: It's a place where you can ...

MEMO

NEW WORDS

- start - get-together - meet - tell - ask - try - have fun - work hard
- rollerblades - kite - place
- late - real - own
- already - then
- What do you mean?

AND NOW... THINK!

1. Observe ces exemples :

Let's go to the park.
What about going to the cinema?
Why don't we read comics?

Complète maintenant les phrases suivantes :

What about est suivi de : ....

Let's est suivi de : ....

Why est suivi d'une forme ❑ négative ❑ interrogative ❑ interro-négative.

Remarque : la personne qui parle utilise *Let's (let us)* pour faire une suggestion qui la concerne aussi.

2. *John wants to try his new kite.*

| *John wants* | .... | *try his new kite.* |

• **Ajoute entre les deux cadres le mot qui crée le lien entre les deux parties de la phrase.**

• **Tu as déjà rencontré *to* dans des phrases comme :**
I go to the swimming pool every Saturday.

Quel est le symbole qui illustre le mieux *to* : ⊗ ou → ?

to marque donc un ....

• **Dans la phrase *"John wants to try his new kite."*, *to* peut-il être représenté par le même symbole ?** .... **Pourquoi ?**

....

• **Quand tu relis un exercice ou un devoir, vérifie bien que tu n'as pas oublié *to* dans ce type de phrase.**

Attention : Dans ces phrases, *to* n'est pas accentué : [tə], donc on l'entend à peine. Respecte bien cette "forme faible" quand tu parles.

at home

memorize

1 Dans le dialogue suivant, replace *Why don't we, What about, I want, I don't want* à leur place. Puis vérifie dans le texte encadré page 30 ci-dessus.

Nelly: Pam, ... going to the cinema?

Pam: Oh no, Nelly, I don't want to sit and watch a movie.

Nelly: .... go to the swimming pool?

Pam: .... to go to the pool. It's too late!

Nelly: What do you want to do, then?

Pam: .... to try my new bike.

Nelly: Okay, let's go then!

read

2 Relis le dialogue page 37 et recopie ces répliques au bon endroit dans les extraits ci-dessous.

Let's go and tell Robin! - Why don't we start our own club? - What about starting a nature club? - Let's start a "get-together" club!

1. *Tracy:* Melissa ....

Hey, what do you think?

Melissa: A new club? Why not?

2. *Tracy:* ....

We love animals, trees, flowers, walking in the woods...

Melissa: But Tracy... There are already two or three nature clubs in town.

3. *Tracy:* ....

Melissa: What do you mean, a "get-together" club?

4. *Melissa:* Tracy, I think that's a great idea! Let's start a "get-together" club!

....!

Little sister: I want to go with you, I want to go with you!

practise

3 Vous voulez organiser votre après-midi avec des ami(e)s : certain(e)s font des suggestions, d'autres ne veulent pas faire certaines activités. Écris une phrase par illustration en utilisant chaque fois une expression différente.

write

4 Tu vas écrire à ta correspondante anglaise qui vient passer quelques jours chez toi et tu aimerais savoir ce qu'elle veut faire pendant son séjour. Complète les questions que tu lui poseras.

Exemple : ... do on Sunday? ➔ *What do you want to do on Sunday?*

.... see?

.... go?

.... visit?

.... go to Paris? The first weekend or the second?

RHYTHM'N SOUNDS

1. Écoute ces phrases et souligne les liaisons.

Ex. : Top of the class.

a) They get up late.
b) A dead pig or a dead bird.
c) It eats it up in ten minutes.
d) They're man-eaters.
e) What about starting a nature club?

2. Écoute ces phrases. Souligne les "h" aspirés et barre les "h" muets.

a) She has got brown hair.
b) Finish your homework. We're leaving in an hour.
c) How many pupils are there?
d) Accidents happen all the time.
e) He's an honest man.
f) And across the hall there's the dining-hall.
g) Are you hungry?
h) Does Fred like history?

EXTRA PRACTICE

PART 1

Fais des comparaisons avec les éléments suivants :

a) trains / planes / fast

....

b) a van / a car / spacious

....

c) a weekend in London / a weekend at home / exciting

....

d) the Sears Tower in Chicago (1,707 ft) / the Empire State Building in New York (1,472 ft) / tall

....

e) vegetables and fruit / sweets and chewing gum / good for you

....

Comparatif d'égalité (aussi + adj. + que)	pour tous les adjectifs *as* + **adjectif** + *as* *He is as tall as his brother.* *The book is as interesting as the film.*	
Comparatif de supériorité (plus + adj. + que)	Pour les adjectifs courts d'une syllabe, ou ceux de 2 syllabes terminés en *-y*, *-er*... **adjectif** *-er* + *than* *He is taller than Fred.* Attention : *big* → *bigger* *funny* → *funnier*	Pour les adjectifs longs : 2 syllabes et plus *more* + **adjectif** + *than* *The book is more interesting than the film.*

Comparatifs irréguliers : *good* → *better* ; *bad* → *worse.*

PART 2

Tu vas entendre six personnes. De quelle publicité parlent-ils ? Note les mots qui t'ont aidé(e) à décider.

	words that helped me	ad n° ...
1st		
2nd		
3rd		
4th		
5th		
6th		

LET'S HAVE FUN!

Peux-tu compléter le tableau ?

Baker Street:

Name					
Pet					
Hobby					

a) Mr Birt hasn't got a pet.

b) There is a cat at number 20.

c) Miss Dudd's dog lives between the rabbit and the canary.

d) The woman with the rabbit plays golf every Sunday.

e) There are four pets in Baker Street: a cat, a dog, a canary and a rabbit.

f) Mrs Evans has got a rabbit.

g) Miss Dudd reads love stories.

h) There is no pet at number 18.

i) The pet at number 12 is a rabbit.

j) Mr Charles is a tennis player.

k) Mrs Abraham likes reading detective stories to her cat.

l) Mrs Abraham's neighbour watches a lot of television.

LEARN YOUR WORDS

Retrouve dans la grille la traduction des verbes suivants et note-les à côté :

nager : ....
prendre plaisir à : ....
chercher : ....
tuer : ....
construire : ....
ressembler : ....
oublier : ....
bavarder : ....
détester : ....
dormir : ....
vivre : ....
manger : ....
grimper : ....
sauter : ....
aider : ....

M	A	D	L	B	U	I	L	D
I	C	F	O	R	G	E	T	S
W	L	O	O	K	...	F	O	R
S	I	C	K	L	H	W	E	V
A	M	N	...	I	E	U	T	J
Z	B	T	L	V	L	X	A	U
T	T	A	I	E	P	L	H	M
A	I	H	K	S	L	E	E	P
E	X	C	E	N	J	O	Y	A

MAINTENANT TU SAIS

Lesson 1
- Parler des habitudes
- Interroger et répondre sur les habitudes

Polar bears eat fish.
Do they sleep in the snow?
Yes, they do./No they don't.
Where do they sleep? In the snow.

Lesson 2
- Exprimer la fréquence d'une action
- Interroger sur la fréquence d'une action
- Parler des goûts de quelqu'un

She never chats in class.
Do you often forget your homework?
She loves surfing the Internet.

Lesson 3
- Dire ce que l'on veut faire
- Faire des suggestions

He wants to try his new kite.
Let's go!
What about starting a nature club?
Why don't we go to the swimming pool?

Extra practice
- Révision du comparatif de supériorité.
- Repérer les mots accentués qui portent l'information essentielle.

UNIT 3

LESSON 1

at school

2 Listen and speak

- Le texte enregistré reproduit ici doit être caché pendant l'exercice d'écoute.
- Il te servira de modèle, au besoin, pendant l'activité orale.
- Tu pourras en mémoriser quelques phrases avant un contrôle oral ou écrit.

1. There was a swimming pool and a public library in the sixties.
2. In the sixties, there was a Youth club, but there wasn't a public library.
3. It was a very small village in the sixties: there weren't any shops!
4. There were two schools in the sixties.
5. Oh no, there wasn't a stadium, but there was a football club.
6. There weren't any cinemas in the sixties, but there were two restaurants.

3 Listen and understand

a) Look at picture one and remember.

Class: The three heroes want to ...
A get-together club is ...

b) Say all you know about Robin Hood... or ask your teacher questions!

Class: Robin Hood was ... / Who was Robin Hood? / How do you say “hors-la loi” in English?

c) Look at picture 3 now and comment!

Class: It's ... / She was ...

Bettmann / Corbis (Sygma)

d) Listen to part one and tick the words you hear, then listen again and recap.

Class: Melissa remembers a ... in the .... There were lots of ... and there was a ... too. ...

- ❑ wards
- ❑ woods
- ❑ roots

- ❑ dotage
- ❑ old age
- ❑ cottage

- ❑ bart
- ❑ barn
- ❑ ban

- ❑ ducks
- ❑ docks
- ❑ bucks

e) Listen to the dialogue and link the adjectives to the corresponding people, animal or things.

nice

sweet

old

empty

delicious

not big

quiet

beautiful

funny

tall

little

f) Listen again and check, then describe.

Pupil 1: The cottage was old.
Pupil 2: It was beautiful.
...

g) Now, answer your teacher's questions.

Teacher: What was the man like?
Pupil 1: He was ....
Pupil 2: With ... hair.
Pupil 3: He was ... with ... hair.
Pupil 4: And he was ....
...

h) Listen again to the end of the dialogue and recap.

MEMO

NEW WORDS

- duck - husband ≠ wife - cook - scone
- beautiful - quiet - sweet = nice - grey - delicious - brilliant
- need - remember ≠ forget
- exactly

empty ≠ full

AND NOW... THINK!

a) Quand utilise-t-on le prétérit ? Complète cette phrase avec les mots : présent / passé.

On utilise le prétérit quand on veut parler d'un moment du ....

sans dire quoi que ce soit du moment ....

b) Remplis le tableau de conjugaison de *Be* au prétérit :

singulier	I he, she, it	....
pluriel	we you they	....

You est donc traité comme un ❑ *singulier* ❑ pluriel.

Est-ce le cas au présent ? ❑ oui ❑ non

at home

memorize

1 Complète les phrases suivantes avec : *there was, there wasn't, there were* ou *there weren't,* puis vérifie dans le texte encadré page 38 ci-dessus.

1. .... a swimming pool and a public library in the sixties.

2. In the sixties, ... a Youth club, but .... a public library.

3. It was a very small village in the sixties: .... any shops!

4. .... two schools in the sixties.

5. Oh no, ... a stadium, but .... a football club.

6. .... any cinemas in the sixties, but .... two restaurants.

read

2 Les phrases suivantes sont toutes fausses ! Relis le dialogue page 47 de ton livre et corrige-les.

a) Her husband was a very bad cook.

....

b) Her scones were disgusting.

....

c) The woman was small with grey hair.

....

d) It was horrible and very noisy.

....

e) There was a young couple.

....

f) There weren't any ducks.

....

practise

3 a) Complète avec *was* ou *were, wasn't* ou *weren't* :

When I .... little, cities .... very dirty because there .... a lot of smoke. That's why I .... happy when we visited my grandparents' in the country. The garden .... beautiful,

with lots of flowers. There .... some ducks too. My granny .... a very good cook and my grandfather .... very sweet to me. It .... a fantastic place! And you know, there .... any teachers because there .... a school!!!

b) Pose les trois questions qui auraient comme réponses les éléments soulignés.

1. *Why* ....

2. *What* ....

3. ....

4 **Relie les colonnes pour former quatre phrases correctes que tu recopieras en-dessous. Utilise obligatoirement les quatre éléments de la deuxième colonne.**

there was •	• lots of •	• cats •	• in the garden.
there were •	• any •	• trees •	• in the old cottage.
there weren't •	• some •	• ducks •	
	• a •	• little girl •	
		• dog •	

....

....

....

....

write

5 **Tu interroges un de tes grands-parents. Rédige une courte conversation : tu lui demandes de te décrire ton père ou ta mère et la maison ou l'appartement où ils habitaient dans les années 19... . Tu peux tout inventer bien sûr !**

....

....

....

....

....

....

....

....

LESSON 2

1 Get ready

b) How is "-ed" pronounced? Listen to verbs in the past and tick the right box.

	[d]	[t]	[ɪd]
travelled			
worked			
composed			
painted			
listened			

	[d]	[t]	[ɪd]
started			
stopped			
danced			
played			
recorded			

2 Listen and speak

a) Listen and fill in the grids.

Interview n° 1 :

Name:
Place of birth:
Date of birth:
Job: *painter*
Started at the age of...:
Worked hard: *From* .... *to* ....
Date of first exhibition:

Interview n° 2 :

Name:
Place of birth:
Date of birth:
Job: *drummer*
Started at the age of...:
Favourite music:
Date of first concert:

- Le texte enregistré reproduit ici doit être caché pendant l'exercice d'écoute.
- Il te servira de modèle, au besoin, pendant l'activité orale.
- Tu pourras en mémoriser quelques phrases avant un contrôle oral ou écrit.

Interviewer: Good evening everybody. Please welcome our two young artists, Lydia and Danny. Lydia, when and where were you born?
Lydia: I was born in Manchester, on July 17th, 1981.
Interviewer: When did you start painting?
Lydia: Oh! I started painting when I was six... and I never stopped!
Interviewer: At six! What did you paint when you were six?

Lydia: I painted things, objects, animals... for fun! But I worked really hard from 1995 to 2000. I was at Art school you see...
Interviewer: When was your first exhibition?
Lydia: In 1998, when I was 17.
Interviewer: Now, Danny, when and where were you born?
Danny: I was born in Hong Kong, on September 28th 1983.
Interviewer: When did you start playing the drums?
Danny : I started when I was two, but I started working hard when I was 10.
Interviewer: What style of music do you play?
Danny : I play lots of different styles... but I like jazz best.
Interviewer: When was your first concert?
Danny : In July 2001! It was great.
Interviewer: Thank you and good luck to our two young artists.

c) Now speak! Role-play.

• You are the interviewer. Prepare your questions.

....

....

....

....

• You are the artist. Choose your personality: draw a circle round your choices and fill in the blanks.

Name: Ludmilla - Howard - Mary - Winston - Rebecca - Gary

Place of birth: London - New York - Sydney - Ottawa - San Francisco - Glasgow

Date of birth: 21/03/84 - 15/01/81 - 12/06/83 - 28/10/85 - 13/12/82 - 22/08/80

Job: dancer - painter - guitar player - drummer

Started dancing...: at the age of .... / when I was ....

Worked hard: from .... to ....

First ballet, exhibition, concert: last week / month / year - in .... - when I was ....

3 Read and understand

a) Look at the photo and read the title. Say all you know about this man (name, job, nationality...) or ask your friends questions about him.

b) Scan the article, looking for the answers to your questions. Tell the class.

c) Read the article and underline all the words you know or recognize, then note down the information in the time-chart.

December 9, 1980

LENNON IS DEAD

Yesterday in New York, a madman assassinated John Lennon, the world-famous singer-songwriter.

Millions of fans all around the world watched in horror as the reporter announced the news on television.

John Lennon was born on October 9, 1940 in Liverpool, England. From 1960 to 1970, he played with the Beatles, the most successful rock group in history. The Beatles travelled all around the world from 1963 to 1970 and they played in hundreds of different places. Then, in 1970, the Beatles separated. At the time, they didn't explain why.

Lennon married Yoko Ono in 1969 and he moved to the United States with his family. He composed and recorded songs like *I Don't Want to Be a Soldier* and the very famous song *Imagine* during the 70s.

For the whole world, Lennon symbolized peace and love.

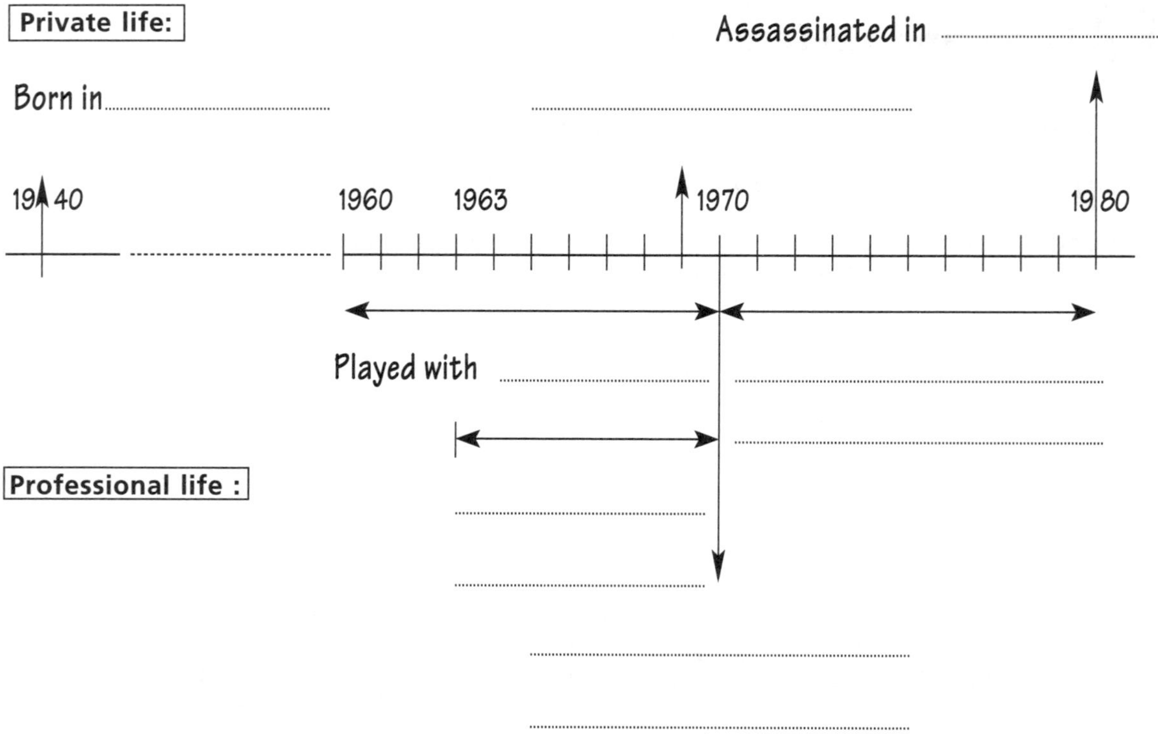

d) With the help of your time-chart, recap Lennon's life.

e) Prepare four questions about Lennon and the Beatles, then quiz your friends. Use :

What? When? Who? Where? Why?

....

....

....

....

....

MEMO

NEW WORDS

- singer - painter - dancer - guitar player - drummer - songwriter
- song - drums - portrait - madman - exhibition
- welcome - travel - move - record - assassinate - separate - marry - start (+ V. ing) ≠ stop (+ V. ing)
- famous - successful
- yesterday - last week

all around the world

AND NOW... THINK!

1. Les énoncés au prétérit comportent le plus souvent des indicateurs de temps. Relis les interviews page 44 ci-dessus ou l'article *"Lennon is dead"*, page 45, et note ici quelques exemples d'indicateurs de temps :

....

....

2. *"I worked hard." - " I didn't work hard." - "Did you work hard?"*

Souligne la marque du prétérit dans chacune de ces phrases.

Que remarques-tu ?

....

➤ **Souviens-toi :** Il n'y a qu'une seule marque du temps par proposition. Quand il y a un auxiliaire (ou opérateur), c'est lui qui la porte.

3. Les verbes ci-dessous sont classés suivant la prononciation de la terminaison *"-ed"* du prétérit des verbes réguliers. Quelles règles peux-tu en déduire ?

[d]	[t]	[ɪd]
played	watched / washed	painted
married	locked	recorded
composed	stopped	
travelled	missed	
moved	laughed	
joined		

- Après les sons-voyelles, on prononce [.........]
- Après les sons-consonnes comme [k], [p], [s], [f] [ʃ], on prononce [.........]
- Après les sons-consonnes [t] et [d], on prononce [.........]
- Après les autres sons-consonnes, comme [z], [l], [v], [n], [m]..., on prononce [.........]

4. Compare :

I was born in 1985.

Je suis né(e) en 1985.

....

....

at home

memorize

❶ **Les verbes conjugués au prétérit ont été retirés de cette interview. En voici la liste : *be (born) - start - be.* Sauras-tu les replacer correctement conjugués ? Vérifie ensuite dans le texte encadré page 44 ci-dessus.**

Interviewer: Now, Danny, when and where .... you born?

Danny: I .... born in Hong Kong, on September 28th 1983.

Interviewer: When .... you .... playing the drums?

Danny : I .... when I .... two, but I .... working hard when I .... 10.

Interviewer: What style of music do you play?

Danny : I play lots of different styles... but I like jazz best.

Interviewer: When .... your first concert?

Danny : In July 2001! It .... great.

read

❷ **Dans cet article, sept coquilles (erreurs d'impression) se sont glissées. Sauras-tu les retrouver ?**

December 9, 1980

LENNON IS DEAD

Yesterday in New York, a madman assassinated John Lennon, the world-famous singer-sonwriter.

Millions of fans all around the world watched in horror as the reporter announced the news on television.

John Lennon was born on October 9, 1940 in Liverpool, England. From 1960 to 1970, he played with the Beetles, the most successful rock group in history. The Beatles travelled all around the word from 1963 to 1970 and they played in hondreds of different places. Then, in 1970, the Beatles separated. At the time, they didn't explain why.

Lennon maried Yoko Ono in 1969 and he moved to the United States whith his family. He composed and recorded songs like *I Don't Want to Be a Soldier* and the very famous sing *Imagine* during the 70s. For the whole world, Lennon symbolized peace and love.

practise

3 Relie ces questions à la réponse correspondante.

a) When did the Beatles separate? ....

b) Who composed "Imagine"? ....

c) Did the Beatles travel to the United States? ....

d) Who did Lennon marry? ....

e) Was Lennon born in the U.S.A.? ....

1. Yoko Ono.

2. No, he wasn't.

3. In 1970.

4. John Lennon did.

5. Yes, they did.

4 Complète les phrases suivantes logiquement, avec un verbe de ton choix. Attention : ce verbe doit-il apparaître sous la forme d'une base verbale ou avec la terminaison *"-ed"* du prétérit ?

Help! hier soir : *last night*

1. Yesterday, I w.................... the car and I .... my room, but I didn't .... my homework!

2. Who did you .... ? – My friends Frank and Peter.

3. When did Lennon .... Imagine?

4. I didn't .... to the Beatles' CDs last night, I .... television.

5 Remets les mots dans l'ordre pour former des phrases complètes. Ajoute les majuscules et respecte la ponctuation indiquée. Attention, il y a un intrus par phrase.

1. you / do / did / what / yesterday / do / ?

....

2. I / listened / records / to / watching / old / .

....

3. parents / did / why / phoned / you / phone / your / ?

....

4. match / he / on television / night / watches / the / watched / last / .

....

write

❻ **Écris la biographie de Charlie Chaplin.**

Kipa : Interpress

- Né à Londres en 1889. Ses parents : chanteurs - très pauvres.
- Joue *(act)* pour la première fois *(for the first time)* en 1897 avec son frère.
- Voyage beaucoup puis signe *(sign)* son premier contrat *(his first contract)* à Hollywood en 1913.
- Joue dans beaucoup de films (exemples : *"The Kid"*, 1921 ; *"Modern Times"*, 1935) : beaucoup de succès.
- Déménagement pour la Suisse en 1953.

....

....

....

....

....

....

....

....

He died in Vevey, Switzerland in 1977.

LESSON 3

1 Get ready

a) Listen and link the verbs to their past forms.

go •	• said
buy •	• gave
see •	• woke up
do •	• left
give •	• bought
say •	• went
wake up •	• saw
take •	• came
come •	• took
leave •	• did

2 Listen and speak

a) Close your books. Listen to the chant and write down the verbs your hear.

3 Listen and understand

a) Look at picture 1 and describe it. Then imagine what Mr Bailey says in pictures 2 and 3. Then look at picture 4 and imagine what happened.

Pupil 1: In picture 1, our heroes are ...
Pupil 2: They are having ...
Pupil 3: Last week, three men ...

b) Listen to part 1 and check your predictions, then explain the problem.

Who is  **disappointed?**  **worried?**

Help! a Council house : *une maison qui appartient à la ville*

c) Look at picture 5 then listen to part 2 and speak about Gordon and the painting.

d) Listen again and recap the story.

MEMO

NEW WORDS

- present - kiss - map - burglar - painting
- use - leave - come back - wake up - buy ≠ sell - borrow - show - happen
- lovely - worried - disappointed
- perhaps ≃ maybe ≃ I think ≃ I'm not sure
- I'm afraid... - Never mind!

AND NOW... THINK!

1. Corrige les trois erreurs grammaticales dans ce *chant*. Explique ensuite tes corrections (c'est faux parce que...).

1. – Where did you go ? I go to a shop. ....
2. – What did you bought ? I bought something. ....
3. – What bought you ? I bought a present. ....

1. ....
2. ....
3. ....

2. Relève les verbes irréguliers au prétérit dans le dialogue page 51 de ton livre et écris la base verbale à côté :

....

....

....

at home

memorize

1 Toutes les questions ont été retirées de ce *chant*. Retrouve-les, puis vérifie à la page 50 de ton livre.

Yesterday night, I went somewhere.

....

I went to a shop. And I bought something.

....

I bought a present. And I saw someone.

....

I saw a poor girl. And I did something.

....

I gave her my present. And she said something.

....

She said: "How nice!". And she did something.

....

She gave me a kiss. And something happened!

....

Well! I woke up and it was Monday morning!

read

❷ **Lis attentivement les questions suivantes puis relis le dialogue page 51 de ton livre. Réponds ensuite à ces questions sans l'aide du livre. Tu vérifieras et corrigeras tes réponses ensuite.**

1. What happened last week?

Mr Bailey ....

2. What did the three men do last week?

....

3. Did he speak to them?

....

4. When did they come back?

....

5. What does Mr Bailey think?

....

6. Who did they give the painting to? When?

....

practise

❸ **Complète le *chant* suivant à l'aide de verbes.**

– Last week, I .... someone.
– Who did you see?
– I .... my friend Cindy. And she gave me something.
– What did she .... you?
– She .... me a plane ticket. And I .... somewhere.
– Where did you go?
– I .... to Mexico. And I .... something for you.
– What did you buy?
– I .... a guitar. Look!

❹ **Ton copain te raconte la fin du film policier que tu n'as pas pu voir hier soir... mais tu l'interromps tout le temps par des questions.**

Exemple : *Your friend:* He...
You: What did he do?

Your friend: And the police took...
You: ....

Your friend: The gangsters had...

You: ....

Your friend: But the detective bought...

You: ....

Your friend: So his secretary said...

You: ....

Your friend: And everybody went...

You: ....

5 Invente des questions qui pourraient correspondre aux réponses suivantes. Attention : tu devras poser soit des questions ouvertes (*Wh- questions :* qui commencent par un mot interrogatif), soit des questions fermées (*Yes-No questions* : qui commencent par un auxiliaire ou opérateur).

1. .... yesterday?

– A nice present for my daddy.

2. .... last week?

– No, he didn't. He hates football matches.

3. .... last Sunday?

– My friends Frank and Peter.

4. .... last month?

– Yes, they did and they saw their cousins too.

5. .... last summer?

– No, she didn't. She went to Ireland in fact.

write

6 Raconte ce que Melissa a fait samedi dernier. Vérifie si les verbes que tu emploies sont réguliers ou irréguliers aux pages 142-143 de ton manuel.

9 am: dentist
11 am: buy present for Mom
1 pm: lunch with Tracy & Robin at Jimmy's cafeteria
3 pm: Library / borow "~~Jane Eyre~~" "David Copperfield"
5 pm: make cake for tea.
evening: write two letters, learn Geography lesson.

RHYTHM'N SOUNDS

1. *They were* ou *There were* ? Écoute et coche la bonne case.

	a	b	c	d	e	f
They were						
There were						

2. a) Écoute la base verbale et le prétérit de ces verbes et répète-les.

buy, bought — catch, caught — wake, woke — think, thought
see, saw — write, wrote — teach, taught — speak, spoke

b) Maintenant, écoute le prétérit et coche la colonne correspondant au son que tu entends.

	door [ɔ:]	**no** [əʊ]
bought		
caught		
woke		
thought		
saw		
wrote		
taught		
spoke		

HIGHLIGHTS

1. Have a good look at the four paintings and complete.

Someone is diving and swimming in a swimming pool. *n°* ....

The cowboy is breaking in[1] the wild horse. *n°* ....

They are picking, carrying, dyeing[2] and weaving[3] cotton. *n°* ....

They are carrying furs down the river. *n°* ....

They are all working (paintings *n°* ....) except in painting *n°* ....

1. break in : *mater.* 2. dye : *teindre.* 3. weave : *tisser.*

2. Link the three columns.

painting 1 •	• the West Coast •	• the pre-industrialized period
painting 2 •	• the Middle West •	• the leisure* society
painting 3 •	• the Far West •	• industrialization
painting 4 •	• the South •	• the conquest of the West

*leisure : *loisirs*

MAINTENANT TU SAIS

Lesson 1
- Parler ce de qui existait dans le passé
- Demander comment était quelque chose ou quelqu'un

There was a park.
There were some very big trees.
What was the cottage like?
What were the old people like?

Lesson 2
- Parler du passé (verbes réguliers)

The Beatles travelled all around the world from 1963 to 1970.

Lesson 3
- Parler du passé (verbes irréguliers)
- Interroger sur le passé

He woke up very early last Saturday.
Who did you see last week?
Did they come back yesterday?

Strategies
- Deviner les fins de phrases, deviner le sens de mots inconnus ou mal entendus et faire des hypothèses pour mieux comprendre à l'oral.

LESSON 1

at school

2 Listen and speak

b) Listen to extracts and match them with the pictures.

a	b	c	d	e	f	g	h

- Le texte enregistré reproduit ici doit être caché pendant l'exercice d'écoute.
- Il te servira de modèle, au besoin, pendant l'activité orale.
- Tu pourras en mémoriser quelques phrases avant un contrôle oral ou écrit.

Nigel: Melissa... psst...
Melissa: Please, Nigel, be quiet!
Nigel: Melisssa... psst... it's green and long... with lots of legs...
Melissa: Ssh...
Nigel: And it's walking up your back!
Melissa: What?
Nigel: Now, it's standing on your right shoulder... look!
Teacher: Nigel! Are you looking at Melissa's paper?
Nigel: No, I'm not, Miss.
Melissa: Nigel, where is it? I can't see it!
Teacher: Melissa! Are you speaking to Nigel?
Melissa: No, Miss... I'm working...
Nigel: Now, it's crawling inside your jumper!
Melissa: AHHHH!
Teacher: Melissa! What are you doing?
Melissa: I'm... I'm...
Nigel: She's looking for a caterpillar, Miss!

d) Now, speak! Parodies.

Pupil A: Look at the pictures below. Pick one and answer your friend's questions.

Pupil B: Ask your friend questions and find the right picture.

Pupil B: What is she wearing?

Pupil A: She's wearing trousers and a T-shirt.

Pupil B: What is she doing?

Pupil A: She's standing.

Pupil B: Where is she standing?

...

Then, change roles.

3 Listen and understand

a) Look at the pictures and describe them.

Class: Tracy's standing at the door. She's ...

b) Listen to the dialogue and give more details.

c) Read these two columns, then listen again and link them.

What they say...		What they think...
Tracy:	You! Busy!	Very stupid!
Robin:	Get out!	I'm very surprised: you never work!
Robin:	I'm testing my new invention, the little sister disintegrator.	You are a pain!
Tracy:	Very funny.	I often give you money.
Mrs Charlton:	What! Again!	It's my life: I don't want to answer.

d) Now, recap and explain Robin's, Tracy's and Mrs Charlton's reactions.

Class: Robin isn't ... because he is ... . Tracy is ...! She thinks he is ..., but he says he is ... . He is  ... .

MEMO

NEW WORDS

- trousers - dress - leg - back - shoulder - jumper - caterpillar - money
- crawl - stand - wear - carry - scream
- busy - funny
- inside - again
- Get out! - You're a pain! - I'm off...!

AND NOW... THINK!

- **Quand Nigel dit : *"She's looking for a caterpillar"* :**
  - c'est comme un arrêt sur image ❑
  - il mentionne une caractéristique de Melissa ❑
  - ce n'est vrai que pour cette situation ❑
  - c'est vrai tout le temps ❑
  - il s'intéresse à ce que fait Melissa ❑

- **Observe ces phrases :**

  She's wearing a dress. - I'm working. - What are you doing? - He isn't coming this time.

  Qu'est-ce qui s'accorde avec le sujet ?

  ❑ l'auxiliaire *Be*, ❑ le verbe.

- **Dans une question, quel est l'ordre des éléments suivants ? Numérote-les.**

  sujet : n° .... ; auxiliaire : n° .... ; verbe : n° ....

- **Dans une phrase négative, où se place *not* ?** ....

memorize

1 Lis les répliques page 61 et numérote ces illustrations. Complète ensuite les répliques en t'aidant des verbes suivants, puis vérifie dans le texte encadré page 57 ci-dessus.

speaking to - working - crawling - looking at - doing - walking up - looking for - standing on

n° ....

n° ....

n° ....

n° ....

n° ....

n° ....

1. *Nigel:* And it's .... your back!
2. *Nigel:* Now, it's .... your right shoulder... look!
3. *Teacher:* Nigel! Are you .... Melissa's paper?
Nigel: No, I'm not, Miss.
4. *Melissa:* Nigel, where is it? I can't see it!
Teacher: Melissa! Are you .... Nigel?
Melissa: No, Miss... I'm ....
5. *Nigel:* Now, it's .... inside your jumper!
6. *Teacher:* Melissa! What are you ....?
Melissa: I'm... I'm...
Nigel: She's .... a caterpillar, Miss!

read

2 Retrouve dans le dialogue de ton livre page 61 les questions qui ont provoqué les réponses suivantes :

1. - ....
- No, I'm busy.

2. - ....
- Tracy, get out!

3. - ....
- She's reading in the garden.

4. - ....
- No, he isn't coming this time.

practise

3 Ton copain a oublié à l'école la B.D. dont il a besoin pour faire un exercice. Il te demande par téléphone de lui décrire chaque image.

Help! se raser : *have a shave* - s'habiller : *get dressed* - clarinette : *clarinet* - descendre : *go downstairs*

4 **Tu as mal entendu les phrases suivantes. Pose les questions pour obtenir les renseignements qui te manquent.**

a) I'm ... with John.

b) He's reading a ...

c) She's ... in the garden.

d) They're looking for a ...

write

5 **Décris ces images :**

LESSON 2

2 Listen and speak

d) Now, speak!
Look at the illustrations and act out the dialogues in pairs.

You: Can I ...? / I'd like to ...
Your partner: Yes/OK, you ..., but you ... / No, you ....

① 

② 

③ 

④ 

- Le texte enregistré reproduit ici doit être caché pendant l'exercice d'écoute.
- Il te servira de modèle, au besoin, pendant l'activité orale.
- Tu pourras en mémoriser quelques phrases avant un contrôle oral ou écrit.

Pam: Mum, I'd like to organize a big party for Jenny's birthday.
Mum: That's a good idea..., but on one condition: you must tidy up your room first.
Pam: OK, OK... Now, I can make two or three cakes... and... er... can you buy some coke and soda, please?
Mum: All right...
Pam: And... er... can we have a bonfire in the garden? With some music, so we can dance and...
Mum: A bonfire!! Pam! You know we can't have bonfires in the garden! It's too dangerous!
Pam: OK, OK... What about some fireworks then? Can you buy some?
Mum: Pam! Fireworks are very expensive...
Pam: Well... I can get some money, I can baby-sit or I can do a paper round...
Mum: Pam! Fireworks are very expensive and very dangerous too: you mustn't play with fireworks at your age!
Pam: What can I do then? It's no fun!

3 Read and understand

a) Say all you know about these celebrations in English-speaking countries (dates, countries, songs, poems, traditions, etc.), or ask your teacher questions.

New Year's Eve
Valentine's Day
St Patrick's Day
April Fool's Day
Easter
Independence Day
Hallowe'en
Guy Fawkes Night
Thanksgiving
Christmas

b) Highlight the celebrations hidden in the grid in different colours, then highlight the corresponding sentences in the same colours.

- You can organize an egg-hunt.
- You mustn't forget to buy a turkey and bake a pumpkin pie.
- You can light fireworks but you must be over 16.
- You mustn't sign your card: it must be anonymous.
- You can't have a bonfire in your garden: it's too dangerous.
- You must be good... and you mustn't forget to send a letter or an e-mail to Santa Claus.
- You can dress up as a witch or as a vampire.
- You must play a trick on your friends before midday.
- Irish people must wear green and some shamrock.

I	N	D	E	P	E	N	D	E	N	C	E	D	A	Y
R	A	J	D	F	V	B	G	N	N	D	X	A	P	E
E	V	S	T	P	A	T	R	I	C	K	B	C	R	M
T	H	S	C	H	R	I	S	T	M	A	S	R	I	R
S	C	S	O	Y	U	F	J	N	K	H	N	B	L	L
A	H	A	L	L	O	W	E	E	N	D	S	Z	F	P
E	D	C	X	S	Z	Q	P	L	G	N	U	W	O	Q
V	A	W	K	G	U	Y	F	A	W	K	E	S	O	D
T	H	A	N	K	S	G	I	V	I	N	G	I	L	A

c) Link the dates, with the sentences and the pictures.

"A penny for the guy."

"Merry Christmas!"

"Trick or treat."

"Sugar is sweet and so are you."

"Happy New Year."

"April Fool!"

"God bless America."

1

2

3

4

5

6

7

d) Now, recap all you know about these celebrations.

MEMO

NEW WORDS

- bonfire - fireworks - egg-hunt - trick - pumpkin - pie
- tidy (up) - buy - get - do a paper-round - bake - light - send - dress up
- expensive
- Are you nuts? - It's no fun!

AND NOW... THINK!

1. Relie ces deux colonnes :

Celui qui dit :	**Exprime une :**
You can't have a bonfire in the garden. •	• interdiction
You must tidy up your room first. •	• possibilité
I can baby-sit. •	• impossibilité
You mustn't play with fireworks at your age. •	• nécessité

2. Les auxiliaires modaux *can, can't, must* et *mustn't* sont toujours suivis de la ....

3. Lis ces deux phrases :

a) *I want to organize a party.*
b) *I'd like to organize a party.*

Laquelle choisiras-tu si tu veux exprimer un souhait ? a ❑ b ❑
Traduis-les.

a) ....

b) ....

at home

memorize

1 Tous les auxiliaires modaux ont été retirés de ce dialogue. En voici la liste : *can, can't, must* et *mustn't.* Sauras-tu les replacer ? Vérifie ensuite dans le texte encadré page 64 ci-dessus.

Pam: Mum, I'd like to organize a big party for Jenny's birthday.

Mum: That's a good idea... but on one condition: you .... tidy up your room first.

Pam: OK OK... Now, I .... make two or three cakes... and... er... .... you buy some coke and soda, please?

Mum: All right...

Pam: And... er... .... we have a bonfire in the garden? With some music, so we .... dance and...

Mum: A bonfire!! Pam! You know we .... have bonfires in the garden! It's too dangerous!

Pam: OK, OK... What about some fireworks then? .... you buy some?

Mum: Pam! Fireworks are very expensive...

Pam: Well... I .... get some money, I .... baby-sit or I .... do a paper round...

Mum: Pam! Fireworks are very expensive and very dangerous too: you .... play with fireworks at your age!

Pam: What .... I do then? It's no fun!

read

2 La plupart des verbes ont été retirés dans les phrases ci-dessous. Essaie de les replacer tous et vérifie ensuite dans ton livre page 63.

light - organize - sign - wear - forget - have - dress up - play - be (2)

- You can .... an egg-hunt.
- You mustn't .... to buy a turkey and bake a pumpkin pie.
- You can .... fireworks but you must .... over 16.
- You mustn't .... your card: it must be anonymous.
- You can't .... a bonfire in your garden: it's too dangerous.
- You must .... good... and you mustn't forget to send a letter or an e-mail to Santa Claus.
- You can .... as a witch or as a vampire.
- You must .... a trick on your friends before midday.
- Irish people must .... green and some shamrock.

3 Retrouve les verbes suivants dans les phrases ci-dessus.

allumer :....................................

acheter ....

oublier : ....

envoyer : ....

se déguiser : ....

porter (un vêtement) : ....

cuire (au four): ....

practise

4 Complète ce dialogue avec : *must, mustn't, can* ou *can't*.

Chris: This English essay is very difficult, Miss. .... Jenny help me, please?

Teacher: No, she .... You .... do it on your own.

Chris: Why?

Teacher: Because it's a test, that's why. And you .... cheat!

Chris: Oh, Miss!

Help! on your own : *tout seul* - cheat : *tricher*

write

❺ **Tu imagines que tu habites sur une autre planète. Rédige les règles que devront suivre les futurs visiteurs, c'est-à-dire ce qu'il est absolument nécessaire/ obligatoire de faire, ce qu'il est interdit de faire et ce qu'ils ont la permission de faire.**

Exemple : *You must... You mustn't... You can...*

....

....

....

....

....

LESSON 3

2 Listen and speak

- Le texte enregistré reproduit ici doit être caché pendant l'exercice d'écoute.
- Il te servira de modèle, au besoin, pendant l'activité orale.
- Tu pourras en mémoriser quelques phrases avant un contrôle oral ou écrit.

Citizen 1: So, you want to modernize the village... What are you going to do?
Councillor: First, we're going to close down the old factory.
Citizen 1: What for?
Councillor: To build a sports centre.
Citizens: Good! Excellent idea!
Councillor: We're going to knock down the greengrocer's.
Citizen 2: Demolish the greengrocer's! But... what for?
Councillor: To build a supermarket.
Citizens: Well... why not... we need a supermarket...
Councillor: And we're going to cut down some trees in the park.
Citizen 3: What for?
Councillor: To build a car park.
Citizens: 'Seems a shame!

3 Listen and understand

a) What's going to happen? Look at the comic strip and comment or make guesses.

You: In picture 1, the 3 heroes are going to ...

b) Listen and check your predictions.

c) Read these two columns, then listen again and link them.

What they say...:	How they feel...:
'Seems a shame. •	• surprised 
Where are they going to live? •	• excited 
In an old people's home! •	• worried 
Incredible! •	• shocked 
Come on, children, quick! •	

d) Now recap and justify:

You: ... is shocked because ...

e) Listen again to the end. They are all going to the library. What for?

AND NOW... THINK!

1. ***They are going to knock down the cottage.***

- À quel temps est conjugué *go* ? ....

- L'action : *"knock down the cottage"* se situe : ❑ dans le présent ❑ dans l'avenir.

- Dans cette phrase il y a donc un mouvement du présent vers l'avenir : celui qui parle a vu un bulldozer ou est en possession d'informations et ceci lui permet maintenant de prédire l'avenir. Souligne les mots qui indiquent ce "mouvement vers".

2. Trouve dans le texte encadré page 68 une question qui permet d'interroger sur le but :

....

Note la réponse et souligne le mot qui introduit la subordonnée de but :

....

MEMO

NEW WORDS

- fall - close down - cut down - knock down = demolish - need - build
- excited - worried - pleased - shocked - incredible
- builder - painting - greengrocer's - car park
- Have a quick look at - 'Seems a shame.

at home

memorize

1 Le débat à la mairie a été recopié dans le désordre. Heureusement, tu as le résumé des projets pour remettre de l'ordre :

They are going to close down the factory to build a sports centre, they are going to knock down the greengrocer's to build a supermarket and they are going to cut down some trees in the park to build a car park.

Mets entre crochets les phrases mal placées et flèche-les à leur place. Puis vérifie dans le texte encadré page 68 ci-dessus.

Citizen 1: So, you want to modernize the village... What are you going to do?
Councillor: First, we're going to close down the old factory.
Citizen 1: What for?
Councillor: To build a car park.
Citizens: Good! Excellent idea!
Councillor: We're going to cut down some trees in the park.
Citizen 2: Demolish the greengrocer's! But... what for?
Councillor: To build a supermarket.
Citizens: Well... why not... we need a supermarket...
Councillor: And we're going to knock down the greengrocer's.
Citizen 3: What for?
Councillor: To build a sports centre.
Citizens: 'Seems a shame!

read

2 Voici un résumé du dialogue page 65 de ton livre. Peux-tu dire pour chaque phrase du résumé si l'affirmation est exacte *(true)* ou fausse *(false)* ? Souligne les erreurs en rouge et rétablis la vérité en dessous.

Exemple : The children meet Miss Parker at the cottage. *true* ❑ *false* ☒
the newsagent's

a) The man says that some builders from London are going to build the Baileys' cottage.
true ❑ *false* ❑ ....

b) They want to build a warehouse.
true ❑ *false* ❑ ....

c) Tracy is worried about the Baileys.
true ❑ *false* ❑ ....

d) Robin thinks they are going to put the Baileys in an old people's home.
true ❑ *false* ❑ ....

e) Melissa says they are going to call Mr and Mrs Bailey.
true ❑ *false* ❑ ....

f) Miss Parker has a look at the painting.
true ❑ *false* ❑ ....

g) She is very surprised because she thinks it's the original.
true ❑ *false* ❑ ....

h) They are all going to the newsagent's to check in an encyclopedia.
true ❑ *false* ❑ ....

practise

3 Complète les phrases avec les bases verbales suivantes en exprimant chaque fois l'intention et le but :

phone - demolish - sell - buy - work hard

Exemple : *He's going* ***to*** *phone her* ***to*** *invite her to his party.*

They .... make a cake.

He .... build a supermarket.

She .... make money.

I .... get good marks.

4 Voici quatre questions. Recopie chacune avant la réponse qui lui correspond.

1. *What is she going to buy?*
2. *What are they going to sell?*
3. *What is he going to buy a new car for?*
4. *What is he going to sell his store for?*

– .... ?

– A new dress.

– .... ?

– To drive to Canada.

– .... ?

– They're going to sell their house.

– .... ?

– To buy a motel in Kansas.

write

❺ **Imagine que tu écris avec ta classe une lettre à la mairie de ta ville ou de ton village pour demander des explications et poser des questions sur le projet de rénovation. Certains changements prévus ne vous plaisent pas et, de plus, vous tenez à savoir ce qui va se passer (par ex. : Allez-vous fermer la piscine ?). Prépare cinq questions.**

....

....

....

....

....

RHYTHM'N SOUNDS

1. Écoute les questions et note si leur terminaison est ascendante ou descendante en dessinant ↗ ou ↘.

a) Are you coming?
b) What is she doing?
c) Is Robin going with you?
d) What are you going to do?
e) Are you speaking to Nigel?
f) What is she wearing?
g) Can you buy some?

Entraîne-toi à les dire avec une intonation correcte. Quelles conclusions peux-tu tirer ?

....

....

2. Écoute les mots suivants et souligne la syllabe accentuée.

demolish - cottage - incredible - original - warehouse - painting - surprised - excited

3. Souligne *can / can't* dans les phrases suivantes lorsqu'il est accentué.

Ex. : Can I go out? Yes, you <u>can</u>.

1. – I can see two boys.
– I can't.
2. Be a good boy if you can.
3. He can be good... sometimes.
4. If you can come, that'll be great.
5. Tell me if you can or not.
6. – Can I go to Jill's birthday party Mum?
– No, you can't, you're too young.

EXTRA PRACTICE

PART 1

Read the letter and fill in the chart. Use the symbols ♥ or ~~♥~~.

	Jami		Roy	
sports				
hobbies				
food				
colours	green			

PART 2

Présent *Be -ing*	**Présent simple**
	 Roy
They're painting a wall.	*Roy plays the flute.*
Avec le présent *Be -ing*, **celui qui parle s'intéresse au sujet grammatical** : les enfants. Ici, il décrit leur activité en un point de son déroulement, comme un arrêt sur image. Ce qu'il dit a **un lien avec la situation.**	Avec le présent simple, **on s'intéresse au fait lui-même** : jouer de la flûte. Ici, c'est une manière de **caractériser le sujet** grammatical (*Roy is a flautist*) : **on peut dire cela à n'importe quel moment.**

Écris ces phrases dans la bulle correspondante.
"Oh yes, we work very hard. We do our homework every day."
"Sorry, we can't come now. We're doing our homework."

HIGHLIGHTS

1. What can you do during the dinner break or after school in a British school?

....

....

2. Choose a club or programme and justify your choice.

I want to join the ... because I like / I love / I am good at ... / I can ... / It's fun to ...

....

....

3. Your friend is interested in The Duke of Edinburgh Award. Give him the following information:

How old do you have to be to take part in the Duke of Edinburgh Award?

....

What qualities does the programme develop?

....

What activities can you do?

....

4. Girl Guides. Read the sentences and write down the number of the corresponding guide rule.

E.g.: A guide is always ready to help. *Rule 2*

1. A Guide never refuses to obey an order. ....

2. A Guide never loses her cool (her self-control). ....

3. A Guide doesn't waste her time: she keeps busy. ....

4. A Guide never lies: she never says things that are not true. ....

5. A Guide doesn't kill animals or destroy living things. ....

LEARN YOUR WORDS

1. Associe les images avec la phrase correspondante.

a) It's snowing.
b) It's sunny.
c) There are some showers.
d) There's a storm.
e) It's raining.
f) There are some sunny intervals.
g) It's windy.
h) It's cloudy.

1 : ....

2 : ....

3 : ....

4 : ....

5 : c

6 : ....

7 : ....

8 : ....

2. Remplis les blancs avec les adjectifs appropriés.

It's .... →
It's .... →
It's .... →
It's .... →
It's .... →
It's .... →
It's .... →
It's *freezing*. →

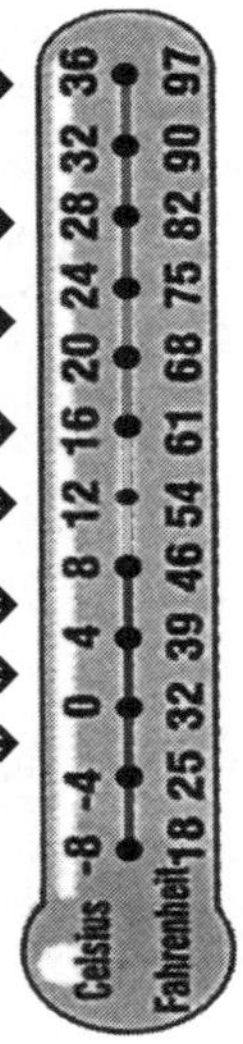

very cold
hot
warm
cool
cold
boiling hot
very warm

MAINTENANT TU SAIS

Lesson 1	• Dire ce qui se passe • Interroger quelqu'un sur ce qu'il fait	*He's writing to his girlfriend.* *What are you doing?*
Lesson 2	• Dire ou s'interroger sur ce qu'il est possible ou impossible de faire • Dire ce qu'il est nécessaire de faire • Interdire quelque chose • Dire ce que l'on souhaite faire	*I can make two or three cakes.* *Can you buy some, please?* *You must tidy up your room first.* *You mustn't play with fireworks.* *I'd like to organize a party.*
Lesson 3	• Parler des intentions de quelqu'un • Interroger sur les intentions • Demander dans quel but on va faire quelque chose et répondre	*They're going to knock down Rose Cottage.* *What are they going to do?* *What for?* *To build a warehouse.*
Extra practice	• Comparer les deux présents	

UNIT 5
LESSON 1

2 Listen and speak

- Le texte enregistré reproduit ici doit être caché pendant l'exercice d'écoute.
- Il te servira de modèle, au besoin, pendant l'activité orale.
- Tu pourras en mémoriser quelques phrases avant un contrôle oral ou écrit.

Miss Farrow: Now, class. Imagine you are going on holiday to one of these places. Your friends must guess where you are going. Isabel, you're first.
Class: Isabel, will you need a cagoule?
Isabel: Yes, I will. It often rains there.
Class: Will you take your fishing rod?
Isabel: No, I won't.
Class: Will you need a backpack?
Isabel: Yes, I will.
Class: Will you take your walking boots?
Isabel: Oh yes, I will.
Greg: So you're going to Hadrian's Wall.
Isabel: Right.

Miss Farrow: Well done, Greg. Your turn now.
Greg: OK, I'm ready.
Class: Will you need an anorak?
Greg: Oh no, I won't. It will be very hot!
Class: Will you take your swimming trunks?
Greg: No, I won't because I can't go swimming there.
Class: Will you need a flask?
Greg: Oh yes, I will! I'll be very thirsty!
Class: So, you're going to the Death Valley!
Greg: That's right.

3 Listen and understand

a) Look at the comic strip and speak about Melissa (Where? What about?). Say all you know about the Baileys' problem, then make predictions about the project: "Adopt-a-cottage".

b) Listen to Melissa's speech once and correct or complete your predictions.

c) Listen again to extracts and write down some keywords. Then listen again and write more words. After that, recap.

Example: ..... **Bailey** .... *lovely* .... **cottage** .... *woods, but* .... **cottage** .... *in* **danger.**

Note : → en **gras**, mots notés à la première écoute. → en *italique*, mots notés à la deuxième écoute.

....

....

....

....

....

....

....

....

....

....

....

....

....

....

MEMO

NEW WORDS

- cross - climb - fly - win - manage (to + B.V.) - become - give back - raise money - save - hope - be worth
- (be) thirsty ≠ hungry - flying
- next ≠ last
- *Apprends aussi tous les objets illustrés page 74 de ton livre.*

AND NOW... THINK!

1. *In 2012, you'll win a gold medal.*

We're sure Gordon will give the painting back.

Souligne le marqueur de temps dans la première phrase. Il indique un moment du ....

Lis la deuxième phrase. Y-a-t-il un marqueur de temps ? ....
(sous-entendu : quand il connaîtra le problème)

Sur quoi Melissa s'appuie-t-elle pour prédire que Gordon rendra le tableau ?

....

➤ **Souviens-toi :** *Will* indique que, pour celui qui parle, les choses sont très probables, mais pas absolument certaines ! On l'utilise pour prédire l'avenir, en fonction de ce que l'on sait du présent ou du passé.

2. Encadre les verbes qui suivent l'auxiliaire (ou opérateur) *will* : à quelle forme sont-ils ? ....

3. *Will* peut apparaître sous deux formes : une pleine : ....
et une contractée : ....
***Will* + *not* se contracte en :** ....

4. *Will you need your sunglasses? Yes, I will. / No, I won't.*
AUX. SUJET VERBE

Observe la formation des réponses brèves et décris-la :

....

Est-elle différente de la formation de toutes les autres réponses brèves que tu as utilisées jusqu'ici ? ....

➤ **Souviens-toi :** Dans les réponses brèves affirmatives, l'auxiliaire (ou opérateur) ne peut pas se contracter car il porte l'accent de phrase.

at home

memorize

1 Écris les noms de ces objets puis vérifie dans ton livre page 74.

....

....

....

....

....

....

....

....

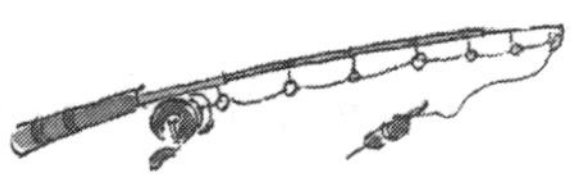
....

....

....

....

2 Complète le dialogue suivant. Lis jusqu'au bout avant de commencer et sois logique dans tes réponses ! Aide-toi du texte encadré page 76 ci-dessus au besoin.

Class: Bob, ... a backpack?

Bob: ....

Class: .... your sunglasses?

Bob: ....

Class: .... your swimming trunks?

Bob: ....

Class: .... your snowboard?

Bob: ....

Class: So you're going to Mt Whitney.

Bob: Right.

read

3 La dernière partie du discours de Melissa est toute mélangée ! Recopie-la dans le bon ordre, puis vérifie page 75 de ton livre.

So next month, on March 6th, we'll have an open day:
I'm sure we'll manage to save the Baileys' cottage.
I hope you and your families will all come and help us.
we'll have a walkathon, a jumble sale, we'll sell cakes and wash cars.
I'm sure we'll raise a lot of money.

....

....

....

....

....

....

....

....

....

....

practise

4 **Complète avec l'auxiliaire (ou l'opérateur) qui convient. Souligne les mots qui t'ont permis de choisir.**

a) Where .... the next Olympic Games take place? - I don't know!

b) Where .... you go on holiday last summer? - Spain.

c) I hope Larry .... manage to finish his boat before the summer holidays.

d) My father .... not like swimming, so he .... never agree to go to Hawaii!

e) Where .... you go dancing yesterday? - To the new disco downtown. The music .... horrible! I .... never go again, ever!

Help! take place : *avoir lieu*

write

5 **Rédige les prédictions de la voyante en un court paragraphe. Utilise les mots suivants :**

first, then, and, after that, finally.

LESSON 2

at school

2 Listen and speak

- Le texte enregistré reproduit ici doit être caché pendant l'exercice d'écoute.
- Il te servira de modèle, au besoin, pendant l'activité orale.
- Tu pourras en mémoriser quelques phrases avant un contrôle oral ou écrit.

- I think we'll have flying cars in the future.
- I don't think so, I think we'll use electric cars.
- There won't be any more pollution in the future.
- I don't agree with you. I think there'll always be pollution.
- Computers will replace teachers in the future.
- I don't think so. I think we'll have computers in classrooms, but we'll have teachers too.

3 Read and understand

a) Read the title and the introduction, then have a good look at the illustrations. Choose one and speak about the future. Ask your teacher for the vocabulary you need.

b) Read the predictions and match them with the illustrations.

A: "Doctors will find a cure for cancer and AIDS, but unfortunately, there will be more and more epidemics." ***n°*** ...

B: "Human cloning won't be illegal any more." ***n°*** ...

C: "Famine will disappear because there will be enough food for everyone." ***n°*** ...

D: "We'll use new sources of energy, such as the sun or the wind, so there won't be any more pollution." ***n°*** ...

E: "New pioneers will go and live on the Moon and on Mars because there will be too many people on Earth, and not enough space." ***n°*** ...

F: "We won't travel any more, but we'll live fantastic, risk-free adventures in virtual reality instead." ***n°*** ...

c) Read the predictions again and underline all the words you know or recognize. Then, infer the meaning of the new words.

- Is it a noun? a verb? an adjective? an adverb?
- Is it similar to a French word?
- Is there a prefix, a suffix? Examples: *un*-fortunate-*ly* / *il*-legal / *dis*-appear
- Can I get help from the illustrations?
- Can I get help from what comes before/after?
- I can be logical.

Examples: No famine **because** → enough food. / Too many people **so** → not enough space. So "enough" means ....

d) Now highlight in green the optimistic predictions, in red the pessimistic ones. Do you agree with these predictions?

Teacher: "Doctors will find a cure for cancer and AIDS."
Pupil 1: It's an optimistic prediction.
Pupil 2: I agree with this prediction.
Pupil 3: I don't agree with this prediction. / I think it's too optimistic! Doctors will never...

MEMO

NEW WORDS

- war - pollution - cure - energy - pioneer - space - reality
- the Earth - Mars - the Moon
- virtual - risk-free - illegal ≠ legal
- replace - use - appear ≠ disappear - agree ≠ disagree
- unfortunately - enough - instead
- I think so. / I think so too. ≠ I don't think so.

AND NOW... THINK!

1. ***In the future, there will be a lot of pollution. / There'll be a lot of pollution.***

- **C'est l'expression .... qui marque le renvoi à l'avenir.**
- **À quelle forme est le verbe qui suit *will* ? ....**
- **Traduis cette phrase. Quelles sont les différences avec le français ?**

- en français, le verbe est .... conjugué au futur.

- en anglais, on utilise *will* + ...

2. ***There won't be any more pollution.***

- **La phrase a-t-elle un sens affirmatif ? négatif ? ....**
- **Compare-la avec :** *There won't be any pollution.*

More change légèrement le sens de la phrase qui devient :
❑ Il n'y aura jamais de pollution.
❑ Il n'y aura pas de pollution.
❑ Il n'y aura plus de pollution.

- **Déduis-en la traduction de :**

"We won't travel any more."

....

"Children won't go to school any more."

....

at home

memorize

1 En t'aidant du texte encadré page 81 ci-dessus, complète ces échanges.

- I think .... computers in our kitchens in the future.
- I don't think so, I think .... robots.
- .... any more forests in the future.
- I don't agree with you. I think .... always .... forests.
- Internet .... books in the future.
- I don't think so. I think .... Internet, but .... books too.

read

2 Retrouve dans le texte page 77 de ton livre les mots ou expressions suivantes :

sans risque : ....

pas assez de place : ....

pour tout le monde : ....

trouver un remède : ....

disparaître : ....

assez de nourriture : ....

malheureusement : ....

practise

3 Voici deux prédictions sur l'avenir du monde. Rédige des prédictions qui expriment des idées contraires. Tu peux trouver deux possibilités pour chacune en utilisant :

not any, not any more, a lot of, more and more.

a) There'll be a lot of forests.

....

....

b) There won't be any more wars.

....

....

write

4 Imagine une ville ou une école du futur. Dis ce qu'il y aura, ce qu'il n'y aura pas ou plus, ce qu'on y fera, etc.

....

....

....

....

....

....

....

....

LESSON 3

2 Listen and speak

a) Listen and fill in the grids:

Trip	Date of departure	Number of pupils
From .... *to*	....	....

 ?	Duration of the trip	Price
....	....	....

c) Role-play. Pupil A.

Pupil B: Go to page 90.

Pupil A: Explain your project (grid 1), then listen to your friend's answers and fill in grid 2.

Pupil A: I want to go from ... to ... on ... with ...
Pupil B: If you take the ..., it will take ... and it will cost you £ ...

Grid 1:

Trip	Date of departure	Number of pupils
From Glasgow to London	15th June	15

Grid 2:

 ?	Duration of the trip	Price
....	....	....

d) Change roles:

Pupil A: Listen to your friend's project and fill in grid 1, then answer him/her (grid 2).

Pupil B: I want to go from ... to ... on ... with ...
Pupil A: If you take the ..., it will take ... and it will cost you £ ...

Grid 1:

Trip	Date of departure	Number of pupils
From .... *to*	....	....

Grid 2:

 ?	Duration of the trip	Price
plane	4 hours	£150 per person
train and ferry	13 and a half hour	£80 per person

- Le texte enregistré reproduit ici doit être caché pendant l'exercice d'écoute.
- Il te servira de modèle, au besoin, pendant l'activité orale.
- Tu pourras en mémoriser quelques phrases avant un contrôle oral ou écrit.

Travel agent: So, you want to go from Dublin to Lille, France on April 6th, with a group of 20 pupils. Let me see... If you go by ferry and by train, the trip will take 25 hours, but it will cost you only £100 per person. Now, if you take the plane, the trip will only take 2 and a half hours, but it will cost £140 per person.
So, ferry or plane?
Miss Farrow: Er... Can you say that all again, please?

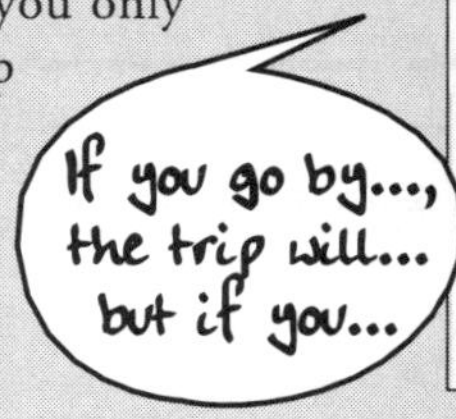

3 Listen and understand

a) Look at the illustrations. Ask and answer as many questions as you can: Who? Where? When? How? How much? How long?

b) Now, listen and write down the answers to your questions.

....

....

....

c) Listen again and draw the route on the map. Note down the flight times and the duration of the flight and of the stopover.

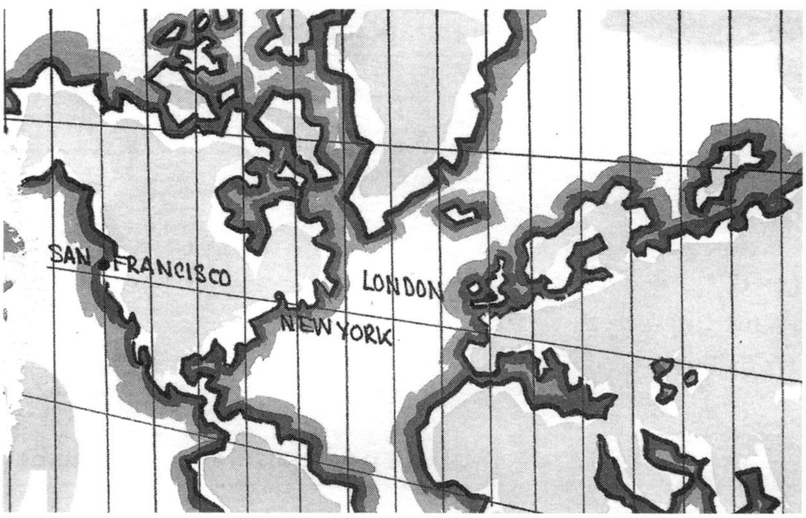

d) Now, check your information: ask and answer questions.

Class: How much will the flight cost if they go on ...?
Pupil 1: It will cost ... for ...

e) Recap.

MEMO

NEW WORDS

- how long - how far - how much
- trip - flight - ticket - price - duration
- during - only - each - whole
- by boat - by plane
- Let me see...

AND NOW... THINK!

1. *Travel agent: "If you go by plane, it will take two hours."*

- **Dans cette phrase, il y a deux propositions, mets-les entre crochets.**
- **Il y a une supposition et une conséquence. Souligne en bleu la supposition et en rouge la conséquence.**
- **Quel mot permet d'introduire la supposition ? :** ....
- **Encadre le groupe verbal de chaque proposition. Que remarques-tu ?**

La .... est exprimée au présent simple.

La .... est exprimée avec *will* + B.V.

- **Comment l'agent de voyage peut-il prédire *"it will take two hours"* ?**

❑ C'est lui qui décide.
❑ À partir de la supposition, il a fait un calcul.

2. Associe les questions à ce sur quoi elles interrogent :

How many *pupils will you go with?* •	• le prix
How long *will the flight take?* •	• le moyen de transport
How far *is it to London?* •	• la durée
How much *will the trip cost?* •	• le nombre
How *will you get there?* •	• la distance

- **Connais-tu d'autres questions en *How* ?** ....

at home

memorize

1 Complète le texte avec les verbes : *go, cost, take,* soit au présent simple, soit employés avec *will*. Puis vérifie dans le texte encadré page 86 ci-dessus.

Travel agent: So, you want to go from Dublin to Lille, France on April 6th, with a group of 20 pupils. Let me see... If you .... by ferry and by train, the trip .... 25 hours, but it .... you only £100 per person. Now, if you .... the plane, the trip .... only .... 2 and a half hours, but it .... £140 per person.

read

2 Quel mélange ! Voici un résumé du projet de voyage des héros. Recopie-le dans le bon ordre en t'aidant du dialogue page 79 de ton livre.

Our heroes will leave on April 13th and come back on Sunday 23rd.
...and they'll have a stopover in New York.
Then, they'll fly to San Francisco...
They won't have time to visit New York...
The trip will cost £1,150.
...and they'll land there at 11.30 a.m. local time.
They'll take off at half past seven in the morning...
The whole trip will take 12 hours.
...because they'll only stop for two hours.

Our heroes will leave on April 13th and come back on Sunday 23rd. ....

....

....

....

....

....

....

....

....

....

....

practise

3 Écris deux phrases au sujet d'Alison et trois au sujet de Bob.

- Alison → work hard at school → get good marks → parents / buy her a bike → ride to school
- Bob → practise a lot → be good at football → become a champion → be famous

If Alison works hard, she will get good marks.

If she gets good marks, her parents ....

....

If Bob ....

....

....

4 Trouve les questions correspondant aux réponses suivantes :

a) ....

- It'll take me two hours.

b) ....

- It'll cost £250.

c) ....

- She'll be 18 (in 2015).

d) ....

- London is about 400 kms from Paris.

write

5 Tu pars en expédition en Afrique. Tes amis sont inquiets. Ils imaginent les problèmes que tu pourrais rencontrer mais tu es très optimiste et trouves toujours des solutions.

Problems :

- have a puncture 
- get lost
- meet a lion

Solutions :

- phone a garage
- look at my compass 
- take a photo
- phone World Assistance on my mobile

Tu peux imaginer d'autres problèmes et/ou d'autres solutions.

Exemple : – *What will you do if you have a puncture?*
– *I'll phone a garage!*
– *What will you do if your mobile doesn't work?*
– *I'll walk! / I'll hitch hike!* (= faire du stop)

Listen and speak - lesson 3

c) Role-play. Pupil B.

Pupil B: Listen to your friend's project and fill in grid 1, then answer him/her (grid 2).

Pupil A: I want to go from ... to ... on ... with ...
Pupil B: If you take the ..., it will take ... and it will cost you £...

Grid 1:

Trip	Date of departure	Number of pupils
From .... *to*	....	....

Grid 2:

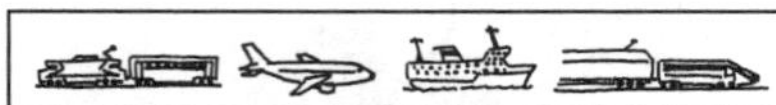 ?	Duration of the trip	Price
plane	3 hours 50	£170 per person
train and ferry	9 hours	£100 per person

d) Change roles:

Pupil B: Explain your project (grid 1), then listen to your friend's answers and fill in grid 2.

Pupil B: I want to go from ... to ... on ... with ...
Pupil A: If you take the ..., it will take ... and it will cost you £...

Grid 1:

Trip	Date of departure	Number of pupils
From Birmingham to Toulouse	25th May	12

Grid 2:

 ?	Duration of the trip	Price
....	....	....
....	....	....

RHYTHM'N SOUNDS

1. *They'll be* ou *there'll be* ?

Écoute les phrases et coche la bonne case selon ce que tu entends.

	1	2	3	4	5	6
They'll be						
There'll be						

2. *Intonation.*

À présent, note l'intonation à la fin de chaque phrase du dialogue ci-dessous. Est-elle ascendante (↗), descendante (↘) ou les deux (↘↗) ?

3. *Sentence stresses.*

Écoute cette conversation et souligne les mots accentués.

Mr Bell: Excuse me, I'd like to go to the station. How far is it?

Mr Holm: It depends. If you go by car, it'll only take you 2 minutes, but if you walk there it will be much longer: half an hour or more.

Mr Bell: Half an hour! That's a long time! Will it be quicker if I go by bus?

Mr Holm: Oh yes, much quicker.

Mr Bell: Is there a bus stop nearby?

Mr Holm: Yes, just behind you.

4. Écoute les phrases suivantes et coche chaque fois la case qui correspond aux sentiments exprimés par le personnage.

1						
2						
3						
4						
5						
6						
7						

STRATEGIES

PART 2. LA STRUCTURE D'UN TEXTE

Relis l'article "*Graffiti*". Les phrases clés *(topic sentences)* sont en caractère gras ; les autres phrases donnent des détails supplémentaires *(supporting details)*.

GRAFFITI

Graffiti, writing or drawing on buildings, causes many problems in certain schools. One problem is that the schools look messy. Another problem is that it costs a lot of money to clean up the walls.

Graffiti "artists" are hard to catch. There are laws or rules against graffiti. But it would cost a fortune to have a guard outside every building. **These laws don't do much to stop people writing on walls.**

A school in Connecticut tried something new to solve the problem. A big rock was placed in the schoolyard just for graffiti. So the students used the rock and stopped "decorating" the school building. A good example to follow!

Quelles sont les phrases que tu utiliserais pour résumer l'article ?

....

HIGHLIGHTS

- **Have a good look at the map and at the photos and memorize the information by asking and answering questions.**
  Pupil 1: How high is Ben Nevis?
  Pupil 2: It's ... high.

- **Play a memory game in groups. Close your books.**
  Teacher: What's the name of the highest mountain in Britain.
  Team A: Ben Nevis.

- **Now it's your turn! Quiz your friends.**
  Team A: What's the name of the most successful group of the sixties?
  Team B: The ...

REVISION TIME!

*Ben Nevis is the highest mountain **in** Britain.*
*The Beatles were the most successful group **of** the sixties.*

Dans ces phrases, souligne l'adjectif et encadre les marques du superlatif.

Qu'y a-t-il de commun ? ....

Qu'y a-t-il de différent ? ....

Comment choisir ? ....

....

Vérifie tes réponses dans le tableau ci-dessous :

Adjectif / adverbe	**court** (1 ou 2 syllabes si terminé par *-y* ou *-er)*	**long** (2 syllabes ou plus)	**irrégulier**
Superlatif	***the*** + adj. ***-est*** ***the*** *high**est** mountain* ***in*** *Britain*	***the most*** + adjectif ***the most*** *famous playwright* ***in*** *the world*	*good → the best* *bad → the worst*

Attention aux modifications orthographiques :
*funn**y**: the funn**i**est*
*big: the big**g**est*

LEARN YOUR WORDS

Recopie les verbes suivants à côté de leur définition.

raise money	disappear	sail 
sell	cross	travel
stay	walk	win
drive 	cycle	fly 

- collect money: ....
- go to the other side: ....
- ride a bike: ....
- go on foot: ....
- go by plane: ....
- go by car: ....
- go by boat: ....
- go from one place to another: ....
- become invisible: ....
- opposite of "buy": ....
- opposite of "go away": ....
- opposite of "lose": ....

MAINTENANT TU SAIS

Lesson 1	• Parler de l'avenir	*I'm sure we'll raise a lot of money.*
Lesson 2	• Parler de l'existence ou de l'absence de quelque chose ou de quelqu'un	*There will be enough food for everyone. There won't be any more pollution.*
Lesson 3	• Imaginer des événements et leurs conséquences	*What will you do if you get lost? I'll look at my compass.*
	• Interroger sur le prix, la durée et la distance	*How much will it cost? / How long will it take? / How far is it?*
Strategies	• Repérer les idées principales d'un texte informatif afin de le résumer rapidement.	
Highlights	• Comparer plusieurs choses en utilisant le superlatif	*Ben Nevis is the highest mountain in Great Britain.*

LESSON 1

at school

2 Listen and speak

b) Listen and tick the adjectives you hear (column 2), then listen again and link the three columns. Now speak about the pictures in your book on page 88.

	• beautiful ❑ •	
What a •	• impressive ❑ •	• Ø
	• small ❑ •	
	• big ❑ •	
What Ø •	• dangerous ❑ •	• view
	• steep ❑ •	
	• fabulous ❑ •	• car
How •	• interesting ❑ •	
	• tall ❑ •	• bridge
	• Ø ❑ •	
It's / It looks so •	• cool ❑ •	• colours
	• wonderful ❑ •	

- Le texte enregistré reproduit ici doit être caché pendant l'exercice d'écoute.
- Il te servira de modèle, au besoin, pendant l'activité orale.
- Tu pourras en mémoriser quelques phrases avant un contrôle oral ou écrit.

a) *Melissa:* Look at that, Miss! What a view!
Miss Parker: It's so impressive!
Melissa: The river looks so small!
Miss Parker: What fabulous colours!
b) *Miss Parker:* What a beautiful bridge! And... look at the boats!
Melissa: How cool!
c) *Melissa:* What a *big* car!
Miss Parker: It's a limo!
Melissa: I'm going to take a photo...
d) *Melissa:* I love this street with all these flowers!
Miss Parker: It's so steep! How dangerous!

3 Listen and understand

a) Look at picture 1: Who? Where? Why?

b) Listen to the first part of the dialogue and tick the right answers:

Gordon knows everything ❑ nothing ❑ about the project.
He'd like to help: Yes ❑ No ❑
He can help: Yes ❑ No ❑

c) Listen again and check your answers then recap.

Class: Gordon knows ...

d) Look at pictures 5 and 6. What's the problem? Who's this young man?

e) Listen and check, then recap.

Class: Gordon ... the painting to ... because ... . Scott is ...

f) Listen to the children's reaction and explain it.

Class: The children are very ... because they ... Yosemite Park.

g) Go to pages 114-115 and listen to the end. Speak about this park.

MEMO

NEW WORDS

- famous - the best ≠ the worst - high - impressive - fabulous - steep
- piggy bank - river - bridge - view - limo - ranger - shoe
- it's worth a lot of money - Have a good time

AND NOW... THINK!

1. ***She's got something in her shoe.***
There's somebody downstairs.
I've got his address somewhere.

- **Associe les deux colonnes :**

something •		• un lieu
somebody •	remplace	• une personne
somewhere •		• une chose

- **Souligne les deux composés de *any* :**

Is there anybody home? I can't see anything.

Ils sont employés dans des phrases : ❑ déclaratives à sens affirmatif
❑ déclaratives à sens négatif
❑ interrogatives

- ***There's nothing in his piggy bank! There's nobody home!***

"No" dans ces composés donnent aux phrases un sens ....

- **Traduis :** *nothing* ....; *everything* ....

2. Lis le texte page 95 ci-dessus et relève cinq formes différentes de phrases exclamatives :

What ....!

What ....!

What ....!

How ....!

.... *so* ....!

Complète les phrases ou entoure les bonnes réponses :

What est suivi d'un .... qualifié ou non par un adjectif.

- Si le nom est au singulier, on a : *what* + {a / Ø} + (adjectif) + nom au singulier.
- Si le nom est au pluriel, on a : *what* + {a / Ø} + (adjectif) + nom au pluriel.

How est suivi d'un ....

So est suivi d'un ....

memorize

❶ Associe les illustrations et les phrases ci-dessous. Reporte la lettre sous l'illustration.

☐ ☐ ☐ ☐

a) I can't see anything.
b) There's nothing in the fridge.
c) I've got my homework somewhere.
d) There's nobody home.

2 **On a supprimé les mots qui introduisent les phrases exclamatives de ce dialogue. Peux-tu les remettre à leur place ? Voici la liste :**

What a (3) - What (1) - How (2) - so (3)

Puis vérifie dans le texte encadré page 95 ci-dessus.

a) *Melissa:* Look at that, Miss! .... view!

Miss Parker: It's .... impressive!

Melissa: The river looks .... small!

Miss Parker: .... fabulous colours!

b) *Miss Parker:* .... beautiful bridge! And... look at the boats!

Melissa: .... cool!

c) *Melissa:* .... big car!

Miss Parker: It's a limo!

Melissa: I'm going to take a photo...

d) *Melissa:* I love this street with all these flowers!

Miss Parker: It's .... steep! .... dangerous!

read

3 **Numérote ces lignes qui résument l'histoire dans l'ordre du dialogue page 89 de ton livre.**

☐ **a)** Scott is a ranger in Yosemite Park.

[1] **b)** Miss Parker and the children are at Gordon's.

☐ **c)** Miss Parker tells him that the Baileys need money to buy their cottage,

☐ **d)** The children are very excited because they are going to visit Scott.

☐ **e)** Gordon is very pleased to meet Miss Parker and the children,

☐ **f)** and that his painting is worth a lot of money because it is an original by Hockney.

☐ **g)** Unfortunately, Gordon hasn't got the painting: he travels a lot so he gave it to his son Scott.

☐ **h)** but he doesn't know why they are here because the Baileys did not tell him anything.

practise

4 **Complète les phrases suivantes avec :**

anything - anywhere - anybody - nothing - somebody

a) There isn't .... in the fridge!

b) What terrible weather! I can't see ....

c) - Is there .... in the cupboard?

- No, there is absolutely ....! Let's go to the shops!

d) - I'm back! Is there .... home?

- Yes, Dad! We're upstairs!

e) Oh no! Where are my shoes? I can't find them ....

f) Listen! I think there is .... in the garage!

5 Construis six phrases exclamatives avec les éléments suivants. Certains éléments peuvent être utilisés plusieurs fois.

how - so - what - a - an - Ø
view - book - place - buildings - trees
funny - fabulous - interesting - beautiful

....

....

....

....

....

....

....

....

....

....

write

6 Écris les noms de quatre groupes de musiciens, chanteurs que tu écoutes ou les titres de films, feuilletons, livres que tu adores ou que tu détestes. Donne ensuite ton opinion en utilisant une phrase exclamative.

....

....

....

....

....

LESSON 2

at school

2 Listen and speak

- Le texte enregistré reproduit ici doit être caché pendant l'exercice d'écoute.
- Il te servira de modèle, au besoin, pendant l'activité orale.
- Tu pourras en mémoriser quelques phrases avant un contrôle oral ou écrit.

a. It's so nice to see you again! You must be exhausted. **Make yourself at home!**

b. Will you be quiet! You're impossible! **Behave yourself!**

c. *Dad:* What a mess! Do you want some help?
Bob: No, it's okay. **I can do it myself.**

d. I bet you're starving children, aren't you? There's cake and pop in the fridge. **Help yourselves!**

e. *Pam:* We're off to Bob's birthday party.
Dad: OK, have a good time!
Mum: **Enjoy yourselves!**

3 Listen and understand

a) Look at picture 1 and answer the questions:
Where are they? What do you know about this place?
Who is this man? What's his job?

b) Listen to extracts and match them with pictures 2, 3, 4 and 5.

c) Listen and check.

d) Why are the kids so happy in picture 6? Make guesses, then listen to the end and check, then recap.

MEMO

NEW WORDS

- exhausted = very tired - lost
- bear - honey - cake and pop - cookie - log cabin
- stay - starve - welcome

AND NOW... THINK!

1. Dans les phrases suivantes, souligne l'auxiliaire ou le verbe en vert quand il est affirmatif, et en rouge quand il est négatif.

They're English, aren't they?
They can stay with me, can't they?
You haven't got a tent, have you?
Bears like honey, don't they?
You went to San Francisco, didn't you?
You didn't see a bear, did you?

Que remarques-tu ?

Quand l'auxiliaire ou le verbe est .... dans la première partie de la phrase, dans la reprise (ou *"tag"*) il est ....

Quand l'auxiliaire ou le verbe est .... dans la première partie de la phrase, dans la reprise (ou *"tag"*) il est ....

Souviens-toi : à une phrase affirmative correspond une reprise négative, et à une phrase négative correspond une reprise affirmative.

Trouve la reprise dans les phrases suivantes :

- *You aren't English,* ....*?*
- *He is a ranger,* ....*?*
- *He gave you the painting,* ....*?*

2. Entoure les pronoms réfléchis puis complète le tableau ci-dessous :

1. *I made the cookies myself.*
2. *Did you make the log cabin yourself?*
3. *Make yourselves at home.*
4. *Kids always enjoy themselves in the park.*

sujet	pronom réfléchi
I	....
you	....
he	*himself*
she	*herself*
we	*ourselves*
you	....
they	....

Que remarques-tu sur la terminaison des pronoms réfléchis ?

- La terminaison est .... pour les personnes du singulier.
- La terminaison est .... pour les personnes du pluriel.

at home

memorize

1 Recopie la phrase qui correspond sous chaque illustration. Vérifie ensuite dans le texte encadré page 100 ci-dessus.

Behave yourself! - Enjoy yourselves! - Make yourself at home!
Help yourselves! - I can do it myself!

....

....

....

....

....

read

2 Retrouve dans le dialogue de ton livre page 91 les phrases dont le sens correspond à celles-ci et recopie-les.

Kids always have a great time in Yosemite Park.

....

Make yourselves comfortable!

....

Have a cookie!

....

Be a good boy!

....

❸ Complète les phrases suivantes avec le *tag* qui convient. Puis vérifie dans le dialogue page 91 de ton livre.

Hey! I bet you're lost, ……………………………………?

They're English, ……………………………………?

My father visited them last year, ……………………………………?

practise

❹ Complète avec le *tag* qui convient :

You're looking for Scott Hammond, ……………………………………?

They loved the park, ……………………………………?

Scott is Gordon's son, ……………………………………?

They can stay with Scott, ……………………………………?

He made the cookies himself, ……………………………………?

❺ Imagine ce que disent les personnages.

1. *Look at yourself in the mirror!*
2. ……………………………………………………………………
3. ……………………………………………………………………
4. ……………………………………………………………………
5. ……………………………………………………………………
6. ……………………………………………………………………

write

6 John a été invité chez des gens très gentils à l'heure du thé. Son petit frère, Tommy, s'est mal conduit. Complète cette conversation en employant des pronoms réfléchis.

Yesterday we were invited to tea at the Brownies'. We arrived at 5 p.m.

Mrs Brownie: Come on in and ....

.... scones.

Mr Brownie: They're delicious, you know.

John: .... ?

Mrs Brownie: Yes, I did, I love cooking.

John: Tommy, please! .... !

LESSON 3

at school

2 Listen and speak

- Le texte enregistré reproduit ici doit être caché pendant l'exercice d'écoute.
- Il te servira de modèle, au besoin, pendant l'activité orale.
- Tu pourras en mémoriser quelques phrases avant un contrôle oral ou écrit.

I loved the story. A girl went on an expedition in the Arctic. She wanted to be the first woman to cross the Spitzberg. She had to walk on the ice for six hours a day. One day, she couldn't start a fire because of the wind, so she had to eat raw fish. Two days later, she couldn't put up her tent because there was a terrible storm, so she had to build an igloo. She was so brave! Nothing could stop her! But after three weeks, she fell down and broke her leg. She couldn't walk any more and she had to ask for help! She was so disappointed! She cried when she saw the rescue team arrive. It was awful!

3 Read and understand

a) Read the title and look at the photo. What would you like to know about the 1906 earthquake? Ask questions. You will find some help in the word bank.

....

....

....

....

....

....

WORD BANK: What time / happen / ?
How long / last / ?
How many / die / ?
How many / be destroyed / ?

b) Read the article and try to answer the questions you asked.

E.g.: What time did it happen?

It happened at ... in the ....

c) Read the 4 paragraphs again. Where did you find the most important information? Now, recap the article.

In the introduction (1st paragraph)? *Yes* ❑ *No* ❑
At the beginning of each paragraph? *Yes* ❑ *No* ❑
At the end of each paragraph? *Yes* ❑ *No* ❑

d) Read the letters written by the people from San Francisco and match the paragraphs and the letters. Complete the chart.

paragraphs	1	2	3	4
names	....	....	....	....

MEMO

NEW WORDS

- storm - rescue team - earthquake / quake - volunteers - inhabitants - fire - fireman
- raw - homeless - devastating - awful ≠ wonderful - brave
- put up a tent - break - fall - cry - wait - get back home - last - destroy - use

AND NOW... THINK!

1. Relève dans le texte encadré page 104 ci-dessus deux propositions dans lesquelles se trouvent *could.*

....

....

• Cherche le temps du texte : il est au ....

could est donc le .... de *can.*

• Tu sais déjà que *can* exprime : ❑ une obligation,
❑ une intention,
❑ une possibilité.

could exprime donc une .... dans le passé.

• À la forme négative, *couldn't* exprime une .... dans le ....

• *Could* comme tous les modaux est suivi ....

2. Relève dans le texte encadré ci-dessus deux propositions dans lesquelles se trouvent *had to.*

....

....

• Le texte raconte des événements passés et datés, il est donc au ....

Relis le texte et réfléchis :

Had to exprime : ❑ une obligation,
❑ une intention,
❑ une possibilité
dans le ....

• Observe maintenant la question suivante et entoure les deux mots du groupe verbal, puis note dessous : AUX. / verbe
Why did she have to eat raw fish?

at home 

memorize

1 Peux-tu retrouver les dix erreurs qui se sont glissées dans ce texte ? Corrige-les puis vérifie dans le texte encadré page 104 ci-dessus.

I loved the story. A girl went on an expedition in the Atlantic. She wanted to be

....

the last woman to cross the Spitzberg. She had to walk on the ice for sixteen hours

....

a day. One day, she couldn't start her car because of the wind, so she had to eat

....

smoked fish. Two days later, she couldn't put up her tent because there was a

....

terrible storm, so she had to build a hut. She was so scared! Nothing could stop

....

her! But after three months, she fell down and broke her leg. She couldn't

....

walk any more and she had to ask for help! She was so happy! She cried when she

....

saw the rescue team arrive. It was wonderful!

....

read

2 Relis l'article de ton livre page 93. À chacun des quatre paragraphes de l'article correspond un des titres ci-dessous. Peux-tu les numéroter selon l'ordre des paragraphes ?

- ❑ City on fire.
- ❑ Helping each other.
- ❑ People killed or homeless.
- ❑ Terrible day.

practise

3 a) Il est arrivé des mésaventures à ces personnages. Complète les phrases en indiquant ce qu'ils n'ont pas pu faire et ce qu'ils ont été obligés de faire.

1. We *had to* spend the night outside because we *couldn't* find the log cabin.
2. I .... walk in the snow because I .... ski at the time.
3. They .... cross the river, but they .... find a boat.
4. The children .... light a fire so they .... eat sandwiches.
5. There was a terrible storm yesterday. They .... go to England by boat. They .... take Le Shuttle.

4 Un marin a eu quelques problèmes en mer. Il répond aux questions des journalistes. Retrouve les questions posées d'après les réponses soulignées.

Exemple : *What did you have to do?*

I had to send an SOS.

1. ....

I had to send an SOS because of the weather.

2. ....

No, I could not use my radio.

3. ....

Yes, I could see the lights of the port.

4. ....

No, I didn't have to fish: I had enough food.

write

5 En décembre dernier, des collégiens en excursion ont été bloqués par la neige. Ils ont dû passer plusieurs jours en forêt dans une vieille maison sans électricité. Imagine ce qu'ils n'ont pas pu faire et ce qu'ils ont dû faire.

Exemple : *They could not ... they had to ...*

....

....

....

....

....

....

....

RHYTHM'N SOUNDS

1. Écoute les phrases suivantes et souligne les syllabes accentuées.

Ex. He <u>ma</u>de it him<u>self</u>!

Help yourself!
I fixed it myself.
Did she go by herself?
Behave yourselves!
Kids always enjoy themselves in the park.

2. Écoute les phrases suivantes et choisis ↗ ou ↘.

Is there anybody home?
What happened?
Are you sure?
What did she have to do?
What time was it?
Did you make the log cabin yourself, Scott?
Why did they have to leave the city?

3. La lettre *"a"* se prononce de plusieurs manières. Écoute les exemples, puis classe les mots suivants dans la colonne qui correspond à la prononciation correcte.

cabin - card - made - happy - accept - state - call - scared - starving - travel - behave - fall - ranger - original - gate - warehouse - park

cat [æ]	car [ɑː]	alone [ə]	Kate [eɪ]	care [eə]	hall [ɔː]

HIGHLIGHTS

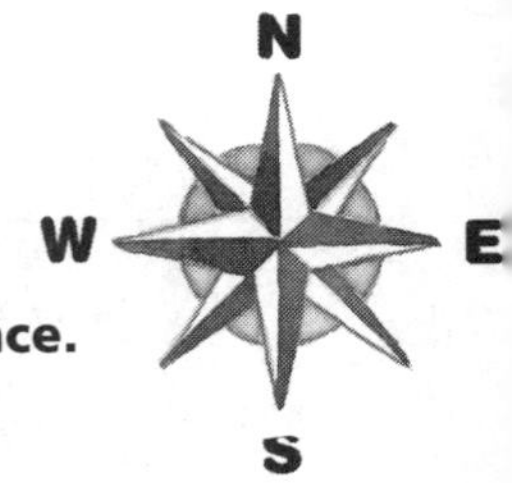

1. Look at the map of the States on page 99 and complete the sentence.

San Francisco is on the West ❑ East ❑ Coast along

the .... Ocean.

2. Look at the map of San Francisco and say where the Golden Gate is.

❑ The Golden Gate Bridge is at the top of the picture facing the Pacific Ocean.
❑ The Golden Gate Bridge is on the right.

3. What's the name of San Francisco's most famous street?

....

4. It's great to visit San Francisco by ....

5. What do they call these beautiful old Victorian houses?

....

QUEEN VICTORIA: Queen Victoria was born in 1819. She reigned from 1837 to 1901, longer than any other sovereign in English history. During her reign, the British Empire expanded and the economy was boosted by the Industrial Revolution.

LEARN YOUR WORDS

1. Enrichis ton vocabulaire. Relie ces deux colonnes et forme des paires d'adjectifs synonymes ou de sens proches.

wonderful •	• calm
frightening •	• pleased
frightened •	• scary
cross •	• fantastic
sad •	• scared
happy •	• starving
difficult •	• adorable
quiet •	• sweet
pretty •	• good-looking
lovely •	• hard
nice •	• unhappy
hungry •	• angry

2. Trouve le contraire des adjectifs suivants en utilisant un de ces préfixes : *in-, im,* ou *un-,* puis vérifie dans ton lexique.

possible • polite • happy • patient • comfortable • sufficient • correct • fortunate

....

....

MAINTENANT TU SAIS

Lesson 1	• Utiliser les composés de some, any et no	*Is there anybody home?* *There's somebody downstairs.* *There's nothing in his piggy-bank!*
	• T'exclamer	*What a view!* *How dangerous!* *I'm so excited!*
Lesson 2	• Utiliser les pronoms réfléchis	*I can do it myself.* *He made the cookies himself.* *Enjoy yourselves!*
	• Utiliser les questions-tags	*You're not English, are you?* *Bears like honey, don't they?*
Lesson 3	• Dire ce qu'il a été nécessaire de faire • Dire ce qu'il a été impossible de faire	*She had to build an igloo.* *She couldn't start a fire.*
Strategies	• Résumer au fur et à mesure pour mieux mémoriser et comprendre une histoire.	

LESSON 1

at school

2 Listen and speak

c) Role-play.

Pupil B: Go to page 115.
Pupil A: You are the witness. You saw five people.
What were these people doing when the Bully Brothers attacked the bank?
Link the columns then answer the sheriff's questions.

Pupil B: What was Miss Rosy doing when they attacked the bank?
Pupil A: She was ...

- Miss Rosy, the school teacher •
- Mr Fatty, the saloon manager •
- Johnny and Tommy, the cow-boys •
- Mr Witty, the barber •
- Mrs Lacy, the shopkeeper •

- • was •
- • were •

- • playing cards outside the saloon.
- • reading a newspaper.
- • sitting outside his/her shop.
- • leaving town on her/his horse.
- • waiting for the stagecoach.
- • coming out of the bank.
- • going into the saloon.
- • going into the barber's shop.

d) Change roles.

- Le texte enregistré reproduit ici doit être caché pendant l'exercice d'écoute.
- Il te servira de modèle, au besoin, pendant l'activité orale.
- Tu pourras en mémoriser quelques phrases avant un contrôle oral ou écrit.

When the Bully Brothers attacked the village, the men were drinking beer and playing cards in the saloon. The women were cooking, two girls were making a fire and the children were playing. Jimmy was playing the violin and the young people were dancing. The sheriff was painting.

3 Listen and understand

a) Look at the picture: what were they all doing yesterday at 7 in the morning? Ask your teacher for the vocabulary you need.

You: Melissa was... How do you say: "se laver à la rivière"?
Teacher: Have a wash by the river.
You: Melissa was having a wash by the river.
...

b) Now, listen to the first part of the dialogue and imagine what happened!

c) Listen to part 2 and check. What happened exactly? Listen again and draw the bear on this picture, then listen to part 3 and check.

d) Imagine the heroes' reactions, then listen to part 4 and check.

e) Recap the story from the beginning.

Class: Yesterday morning, something ....
Our three heroes were ... when ...

f) Listen: "Then Scott arrived..." What did he do? Imagine, then listen to the end and check, then recap the whole story.

g) Listen again to Miss Parker and link the columns.

What she said:	Her feelings:
Oh no! Scott! Where were you? What were you doing? •	• relieved
Thank goodness you're safe! •	• cross
Thank you so much Scott. •	• grateful

MEMO

NEW WORDS

- rock - firewood - noise - stagecoach
- safe - relieved - cross - grateful
- attack - go white - scream - clap - stamp

AND NOW... THINK!

- *[They were dancing] [when the Bully Brothers attacked].*

A B

Cette phrase est composée de deux propositions. Encadre le groupe verbal dans chaque proposition.

Dans A, le groupe verbal se compose de .... + ...

Dans B, le groupe verbal se compose de ....

À quel temps sont ces deux propositions ? : ....

Dans A, c'est .... qui est conjugué.

Dans B, c'est .... qui est conjugué.

Complète : Le prétérit *Be -ing,* se forme avec .... conjugué au .... + ...

- *What was Jimmy doing?*

À la forme interrogative, l'ordre des mots est .... + ... + ...

- *[Jimmy was playing the violin] [when the Bully Brothers attacked].*

A B

Complète : Dans cette phrase, celui qui raconte l'histoire s'intéresse à l'activité de Jimmy (proposition .... : prétérit ....), à un moment du passé qui est précisé : celui de l'attaque des bandits (proposition .... : prétérit ....).

Listen and speak - lesson 1

c) Role-play.
Pupil A: Go to page 112.
Pupil B: You are the sheriff. Ask the witness questions about these people and take notes.
Pupil B: What was Miss Rosy doing when they attacked the bank?
Pupil A: She was ...

Miss Rosy, the school teacher • ……………………
Mr Fatty, the saloon manager • ……………………
Johnny and Tommy, the cow-boys • ……………………
Mr Witty, the barber • ……………………
Mrs Lacy, the shopkeeper • ……………………

d) Change roles.

memorize

1 Complète le texte avec *Be* correctement conjugué. Puis vérifie dans le texte encadré page 112 ci-dessus.

When the Bully Brothers attacked the village, the men …………… drinking beer and playing cards in the saloon. The women …………… cooking, two girls …………… making a fire and the children …………… playing. Jimmy …………… playing the violin and the young people …………… dancing. The sheriff …………… painting.

read

2 Une erreur s'est glissée dans chaque phrase extraite d'un résumé de l'histoire. Retrouve les cinq erreurs et corrige-les. Attention, un changement (de personne, par exemple) peut entraîner d'autres changements dans la phrase.

1. At 7 yesterday morning, Scott was getting dressed when a big bear appeared from behind a rock.

……………………………………………

……………………………………………

2. The kids were looking for wood.

……………………………………………

3. The bear was sitting there, right in front of Robin.

……………………………………………

4. Melissa clapped her hands and stamped her feet.

....

5. The bear didn't run away.

....

practise

3 a) Hier, tu es allé(e) rendre visite à des amis qui campaient. Raconte à un(e) ami(e) ce que chacun faisait lorsque tu es arrivé(e). Écris six phrases.

Laura ....

The girls ....

The boys ....

Mr Johnson ....

Mrs Johnson ....

The cat ....

b) Ton ami(e) te pose deux questions : il/elle veut savoir ce que le ranger et les bébés faisaient.

....

....

write

4 Cinq personnes prétendent avoir vu une soucoupe volante samedi dernier à 6 heures du soir. Un journaliste les interviewe pour savoir ce qu'ils faisaient à ce moment-là. Rédige la conversation.

....

....

Help! *soucoupe volante :* flying saucer
objet volant non identifié (OVNI) : unidentified flying object (UFO)

LESSON 2

2 Listen and speak

b) Have a good look at the illustrations, read the words, then listen again and write the words under the illustrations.

the roundabout - go under the bridge - it's opposite - turn left - the station - go down - the traffic lights - the T-junction - the petrol station - go across the park - go along

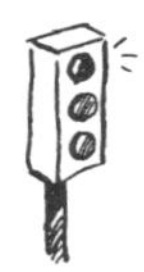

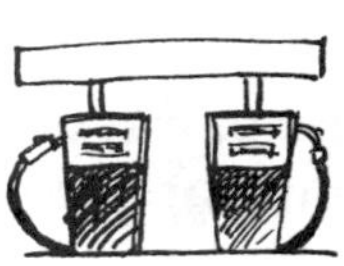

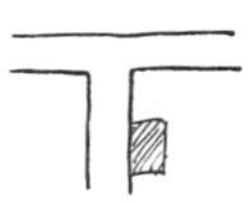

- Le texte enregistré reproduit ici doit être caché pendant l'exercice d'écoute.
- Il te servira de modèle, au besoin, pendant l'activité orale.
- Tu pourras en mémoriser quelques phrases avant un contrôle oral ou écrit.

Brian: Hi Sharon, so our next meeting is on Friday at the museum.
Sharon: OK. I'll take the train. Can you tell me the way to the museum?
Brian: Let me see, from the station, you can't walk across the park, so go down Friar Road. At the traffic lights, turn left, then left again at the roundabout.
Sharon: Left at the traffic lights, then left again at the roundabout.
Brian: That's right. Then turn right at the petrol station. Go along Duke Street. You'll go under a bridge.
Sharon: OK, so I go along Duke Street...
Brian: Right. And at the T-junction, you turn left and the museum is just opposite.
Sharon: What a long way!
Brian: Stop moaning, lazy! See you on Friday at 10 sharp! Bye!
Sharon: Bye!... I think I'll get a taxi!

3 Listen and understand

a) Look at the comic strip. Write down all the words you think you'll hear in the dialogue. If there are some words you don't know in English, write them down in French.

I think these words will be in the dialogue:

Words I know in English:		Words I don't know in English:	
....	....	....	....
....	....	....	....
....	....	....	....
....	....	....	....
....	....	....	....

b) Listen to the dialogue. First, tick all the words you hear from column 1. Then, look at column 2. Listen again and put your hand up when you hear these words in English.

c) Now, with the help of all these words, recap! Listen for more information when you need it.

d) Later in the day, Scott is back at the cabin. The three children tell him about their adventure.

Class: This morning, we were in the tree-house. There were two men...

MEMO

NEW WORDS

- tree-house - path = trail - poacher - river - bushes - plate - bridge - binoculars - bird - jay - roundabout - trafficlights - petrol station - T-junction
- wooden - lazy
- set free - climb - go across - go down - go along
- Stop moaning! - Well done!
- through - up - down - along - across

AND NOW... THINK!

a) La phrase : "*There are two men walking through the bushes*" dit deux choses :

1. *There are two men.*
2. *(The two men are) walking through the bushes.*

• Retrouve dans le dialogue page 105 de ton livre la phrase qui exprime à la fois :

1. *There's a chipmunk.*
2. *The chipmunk is climbing up into one of the cages.*

....

....

• Construis sur le même modèle la phrase qui exprime à la fois :

1. *There are four children.*
2. *The four children are running along the path.*

....

b) Note les prépositions suivantes sous les illustrations correspondantes :

through - up - down - along - across

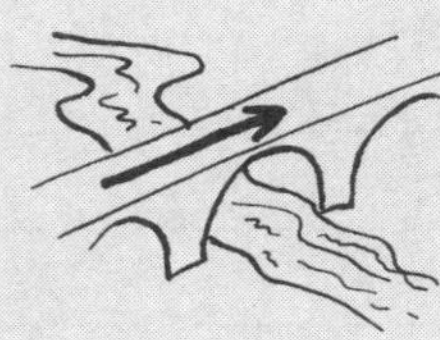

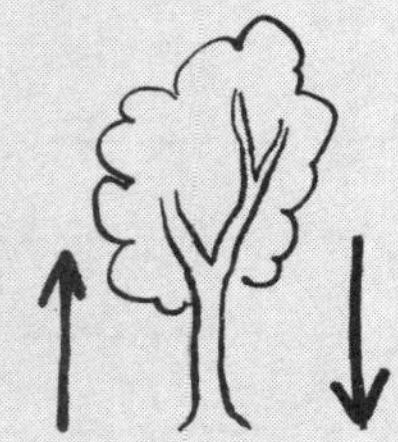

....

at home

memorize

1 Reconstitue le chemin de la gare au musée en numérotant ces phrases dans le bon ordre. Puis vérifie dans le texte encadré page 118 ci-dessus.

n° .... At the traffic lights, turn left,

n° .... and the museum is just opposite.

n° .... Then turn right at the petrol station. Go along Duke Street.

n° .... Can you tell me the way to the museum?

n° .... OK, so I go along Duke Street.

n° .... From the station, you can't walk across the park, so go down Friar Road.

n° .... And at the T-junction, you turn left

n° .... then left again at the roundabout.

read

2 Numérote ces phrases, puis recopie-les dans le bon ordre pour former un résumé du dialogue. Relis ensuite le dialogue page 105 de ton livre pour vérifier.

n° .... Then, they left without the cages.

n° .... They drove down to the river along the John Muir trail and found the cages.

n° .... Yesterday, Robin saw two poachers walking through the bushes.

n° .... They got into their jeep and drove off.

n° .... They opened them and set all the animals free.

n° .... Just after that, Tracy saw a chipmunk climbing up into one of the cages so Miss Parker and the children decided to do something.

n° .... They were carrying cages.

practise

3 Décris cette image de la manière suivante :
Exemple : *There is a man running along the path.*

....

....

....

....

....

....

4 Traduis :

1. Il y a une petite fille qui traverse le pont en courant.

....

2. Je pense que c'était un braconnier parce qu'il portait des cages.

....

3. Il y avait deux chiens qui couraient à travers les buissons.

....

4. Regarde ! Il y a un geai qui s'envole par la fenêtre !

....

write

5 Imagine que tu es chargé(e) de la surveillance d'un parc avec des arbres, un lac et une rivière, des ponts, etc. Tu as des jumelles. Plusieurs personnes te semblent en danger. Décris chaque scène à ton collègue.

....

....

....

....

....

LESSON 3

2 Listen and speak

a) Listen and fill in the grid.

Here are the names: Mrs Peacock - Mr Swanson - Chief inspector - Johanna.

relationship to the Wellingtons	names	clues
....	....	
....	....	
....	....	
	....	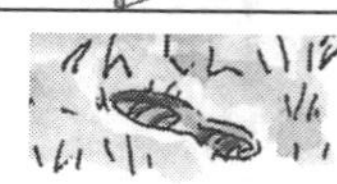

- Le texte enregistré reproduit ici doit être caché pendant l'exercice d'écoute.
- Il te servira de modèle, au besoin, pendant l'activité orale.
- Tu pourras en mémoriser quelques phrases avant un contrôle oral ou écrit.

Chief inspector: So, whose footprint is it?
Detective: It's Mr Swanson's. He is the Wellingtons' neighbour.
Chief inspector: Ah, ah! What about the fingerprint on the safe? Is it his too?
Detective: No, it's Mrs Peacock's, Mrs Wellington's best friend.
Chief inspector: Oh, I see... What about the blond hair? Is it hers too?
Detective: Oh no, it isn't.
It's Mrs Wellington's daughter's, Johanna.
Chief inspector: So, we have nothing to go on!
Detective: We found a raincoat too and we don't know whose it is. It's brand new... maybe...
Chief inspector: Let me have a look... but it's mine!
Detective: It's yours?!
Chief inspector: Yes, stupid, it's my new raincoat! Go back to the Wellingtons' now, and find something!

c) **Now, speak! Role-play: The robbery at the Wellingtons'.**
• Pupil A: Decide who you are: ❑ Mr Swanson, ❑ Mrs Peacock, ❑ Johanna.
Now, the detective is going to ask you questions about some clothes.
First decide: Whose are they? What colour are they? Link columns 1, 2 and 3.

1	2	3
	 • a handkerchief •	• blue
Mr Swanson •	• a scarf • 	• black
Mrs Peacock •	 • a T-shirt •	• green
Johanna •	• a sock • 	• white
	 • a jacket •	• red

• Pupil B: You are the detective.
You found a thread stuck in the safe.

Interview pupil A: Ask his/her name, then ask questions about the five pieces of clothing, and note down his/her answers.

Pupil B: What's your name?
Pupil A: I'm ...
Pupil B: Whose handkerchief is this?
Pupil A: It's ...

 a handkerchief • • ....
 a scarf • • ....
 a T-shirt • • ....
 a sock • • ....
 a jacket • • ....

The laboratory sent you the result of their tests:
The thread is ❑ blue ❑ black ❑ green ❑ white ❑ red.
Ask the suspect this last question, then conclude!

Pupil B: Which piece of clothing is ...?
Pupil A: The ... is.
Pupil B: So ... is guilty. / So, you are guilty!

3 Listen and understand

a) **Look at picture 1 and listen to the beginning of the dialogue. What is Miss Parker going to say? Give as many details as you can.**

b) **Now, listen to the first part of the dialogue: when your teacher stops the tape, finish the sentence (guess what is coming next...).**

Tape: Some builders want to ...
You: demolish / knock down the Baileys'/ their cottage.

c) Now listen: did you guess right? Recap the first part of the dialogue.

d) Predict Scott's answer, then listen to the end. Recap.

MEMO

NEW WORDS

- child = kid - businessman - fingerprint - raincoat - coat - school blazer - jacket - leather - scarf - handkerchief - thread
- worthless ≠ worth a lot of money
- be in trouble
- Of course! - You monkeys!

AND NOW... THINK!

1. a) Observe les phrases suivantes :

The jacket is brown.
Scott's jacket is brown.
Whose jacket is it?
Scott's (jacket).

Complète :

Le génitif se trouve dans une phrase à la même place que le ....

On peut sous-entendre le deuxième nom quand on veut éviter une ....

b) Observe les génitifs ci-dessous et complète :

A : *The ranger's jacket*.
N1 **'s** N2

B : *The boys' cagoules*.
N1 **'** N2

C : *The children's friends*.
N1 **'s** N2

- **Quand le premier nom, N1, est un nom commun, il garde son déterminant.**

Vrai ou faux ? ....

- **Quand N1 est au singulier (phrase : ...), le génitif se forme toujours avec :** N1 .... N2.

- **Quand N1 est au pluriel, deux cas sont possibles :**

➤ **N1 est un pluriel régulier, qui se termine par un *"s"* (phrase ...), alors on a :** N1 .... N2.

➤ **N1 est un pluriel irrégulier, qui ne se termine pas par *"s"* (phrase : ...), alors on a :** N1 .... N2.

2. Lis ces phrases puis complète :

- *Is it **Johanna's jacket?***
- *Yes, it's **hers**.*

- *Is it **Mr Swanson's sock?***
- *Yes, it's **his.***

- *Some builders want to knock down **Mr and Mrs Bailey's cottage.***
- *But it's **their cottage!***
- *No, it isn't **theirs**.*

• ***Hers, his, theirs*** **sont des pronoms possessifs : ils représentent le ou les .... et ce qui est ....**

• **Les pronoms possessifs s'accordent avec ❑ le(s) possesseur(s) ❑ l'objet possédé.**

• **Complète le tableau (quand tu ne sais pas, devine puis vérifie auprès de ton professeur) :**

adjectifs possessifs	*my*	*your*	*his, her, its*	*our*	*your*	*their*
pronoms possessifs	....	....	....	....	....	....

at home

memorize

❶ Réponds à ces questions, puis vérifie dans le texte encadré page 122 ci-dessus.

Who is Mr Swanson? ....

Who is Mrs Peacock? ....

Who is Johanna? ....

Whose fingerprint is it? ....

Whose footprint is it? ....

Whose hair is it? ....

Whose raincoat is it? ....

read

❷ Complète le dialogue avec les éléments suivants :

your father's, the children's, mine, yours (2), my father's, theirs.

Miss Parker: Scott, now the kids are in bed, I've got something to tell you. It's very important. .... friends, Mr and Mrs Bailey, are in trouble.

Scott: What's up?

Miss Parker: Some builders want to knock down their cottage.

Scott: But they can't do that!

Miss Parker: Oh yes, they can. The cottage isn't .... It's a Council house.

Scott: Oh. But I still don't get it, how can I help?

Miss Parker: We're looking for one of .... paintings.

Scott: One of .... paintings?

Miss Parker: Yes. Your father's paintings are .... now, aren't they?

Scott: Yes, of course they're ...., but they're worthless!

Miss Parker: Oh no! You see, the painting Mr Bailey gave your father in England is worth a lot of money.

Scott: Ah, now I get it. They want to sell the painting to buy the cottage. Mmm... OK! Let's have a look in here. Is that what you're looking for?

Miss Parker: Oh it's beautiful! I can't believe it! Scott...

Scott: No. Not another word. It's ....

Miss Parker: Oh Scott! Are you sure?

Scott: Yes, you can have it.

practise

3 Un casse-tête familial ! Corrige ces phrases qui sont toutes fausses en changeant un seul mot, puis traduis-les.

Exemple : Philip's father's sister is his uncle.
*Philip's father's sister is his **aunt**.* (La sœur du père de Philippe est sa tante.)
ou : *Philip's father's **brother** is his uncle.* (Le frère du père de Philippe est son oncle.)

a) Philip's mother's daughter is his aunt.

....

....

b) Your mother's sister's husband is your cousin.

....

....

c) Your cousin's father is your father's father.

....

....

write

4 Tu es le journaliste chargé d'écrire dans le *Yosemite News* l'aventure des enfants à la recherche du tableau et sa conclusion heureuse. Note toutes tes idées et tout le vocabulaire qui te vient à l'esprit puis fais le plan de ton article. Tu rédigeras en classe avec l'aide de ton professeur.

a good-hearted ranger

....

....

....

....

....

....

....

....

....

RHYTHM'N SOUNDS

1. [s], [z] ou [ɪz] ? Écoute et coche la bonne colonne.

	[s]	[z]	[ɪz]
Peter'**s** friend.		✓	
My neighbour love**s** Biology.			
Her brother**s** hate rugby.			
Do you like language**s**?			
She hate**s** homework.			
I love football matche**s**.			
Rick'**s** father.			

2. Écoute les adjectifs suivants et souligne les syllabes accentuées puis répète les adjectifs.

ambitious - hardworking - entertaining - responsible - hostile - horrible - delicious

STRATEGIES

LEARNING TO READ

C • Observe et complète :

This book tells us the story of ***a friendly scientist.***

The friendly scientist *turns into a cruel criminal at night.*

[This book *tells* *us the story of* ***a friendly scientist****]* *[****who*** *turns into* *a cruel criminal at night].*

Who remplace .... C'est un pronom relatif.

Il est .... du verbe *turn into* (se transformer).

Entraîne-toi : Dans les phrases longues ci-dessous, souligne les groupes verbaux et le relatif *who*, puis mets entre crochets la proposition principale et la proposition relative, comme dans l'exemple ci-dessus. Relie *who* au nom qu'il remplace.

- *This book is about a brave dog, Buck, who learns to survive in a hostile region.*

- *It is the story of two naughty boys who live on the banks of the Mississippi river and like playing tricks and skipping school.*

- *This book is about a company of dwarfs who search for a treasure guarded by a dragon.*

LEARNING TO WRITE

PART 3. LES MOTS DE LIAISON DANS UN RECIT CHRONOLOGIQUE

1. Rédige un court texte à propos d'une journée typique de Mr Wild, le gardien de zoo, en t'aidant de la frise ci-dessous et en utilisant des mots de liaison.

has an early cup of tea	*feeds the animals*	*cleans the cages*	*opens the gift shop*	*welcomes the visitors*
6:00	*7:00*	*8:00*	*9:30*	*10:00*

Mr Wild is a zookeeper. Every morning, he does the same things.

.... *he has an early cup of tea* ....

....

....

....

....

....

....

2. Tu peux également te servir des mots *before* et *after* pour raconter une succession d'actions. Observe les exemples puis fais de même.

Exemple : *Before feeding the animals, he has an early cup of tea.*
After opening the gift shop, he welcomes the visitors.

feed the animals / clean the cages

Before ....

clean the cages / open the gift shop

After ....

Quelle remarque peux-tu faire ? Relis les phrases ci-dessus, et regarde la frise de l'emploi du temps de Mr Wild, puis relie les deux colonnes.

Avec *after* •	• les actions sont présentées dans la phrase dans l'ordre inverse où elles se déroulent dans la réalité.
Avec *before* •	• les actions sont présentées dans la phrase dans l'ordre où elles se déroulent dans la réalité.

3. Entraîne-toi : raconte ce que tu fais tous les jours après l'école (ou ce que tu fais tous les dimanches matins par exemple, au choix) en utilisant tous les mots de liaison que tu connais.

....

....

....

....

HIGHLIGHTS

- **What's the ranger's job? Explain, then give two examples of park rules.**

....

....

....

....

- **Your teacher's going to ask you a few questions about the document "Just for kids". Try and answer as quickly as possible.**
- **Would you like to visit an American National Park? What would you like to visit, see or do there?**

....

....

LEARN YOUR WORDS

Don't get mixed up!

Complete the sentences with these adjectives.

exciting • boring • tired • terrified • bored • tiring • excited • terrifying

The speech was so ...., everybody was .... to death.
The supporters are very .... because the match is very ....
This man is too .... to go on. The marathon is very ....
The children were .... because the bear was ....

MAINTENANT TU SAIS

Lesson 1	• Demander ce que quelqu'un faisait à un moment précis du passé • Dire ce que l'on faisait à un moment précis du passé	*What were you doing when the Bully Brothers attacked?* *I was looking for wood.* *The young people were dancing.*
Lesson 2	• Indiquer le chemin • Décrire des gens ou des animaux en mouvement	*Go along Friar Road, then turn right...* *There's a man driving across the bridge.* *There are two chipmunks running through the bushes.*
Lesson 3	• Demander et dire à qui appartient... • Utiliser des pronoms possessifs	*Whose coat is it?* *It's the businessman's. / It's his.* *It isn't the Baileys' cottage = it isn't theirs.*
Strategies	• Choisir un livre, comprendre et rédiger des phrases complexes, utiliser les mots de liaisons.	

LESSON 1

at school

2 Listen and speak

- Le texte enregistré reproduit ici doit être caché pendant l'exercice d'écoute.
- Il te servira de modèle, au besoin, pendant l'activité orale.
- Tu pourras en mémoriser quelques phrases avant un contrôle oral ou écrit.

Chief (officer): So, when did we get their message?
Rescue worker 1: At 8 p.m., sir.
Chief: It's 8:45 p.m. now... er... What did they say exactly?
Rescue worker 1: They said they were lost in a terrible storm.
Rescue worker 2: They wanted to know where they were and where the nearest hut was.
Rescue worker 1: But we can't locate them!
Chief: Did you manage to contact them again?
Rescue worker 2: No, because of the storm...
Chief: I see... Let's hope they were able to put their tents up...
Rescue worker 1: They said they couldn't...
Rescue worker 2: And they said they were very cold and hungry.
Chief: OK. This is an emergency... Let's go! Get the dogs and contact the helicopter unit.

3 Listen and understand

a) Look at the comic strip and say what the children are going to tell their parents.

b) Now listen and note down the letters of the pictures they are speaking about, then listen again and check.

....

c) With the help of the pictures, tell the story in the right order.

MEMO

NEW WORDS

- life (lives) - storm
- lost
- put a tent up - locate - contact
- a couple of days = two or three days
- What's the matter? = What's wrong?

AND NOW... THINK!

a) Souligne les changements quand on passe du discours direct au discours indirect :

Gordon: "I gave the painting to Scott." → Gordon says he gave the painting to Scott.
Scott: "You can have it." → Scott said we could have it.

• Coche ce qui est faux :

- Quand le verbe introductif *("say")* est au présent :
  ❑ il y a ❑ il n'y a pas de changement de temps.
- Quand le verbe introductif *("say")* est au prétérit :
  ❑ il y a ❑ il n'y a pas de changement de temps.

• Quels sont les autres changements dans ces exemples ? ....

....

b) Souligne les changements dans l'exemple suivant :

Mrs Charlton: "Who's Scott?"
Mrs Charlton wants to know who Scott is.

• Complète : Quand on rapporte une question, le point d'interrogation

.... *et l'ordre des mots devient celui d'une phrase* ....

at home

memorize

❶ Rapporte les propos des touristes en détresse, puis vérifie dans le texte encadré page 131 ci-dessus.

a) "We're lost."

They said ....

b) "Where is the nearest hut?"

They wanted to know ....

c) "We're very cold and hungry."

....

d) "Where are we? "

....

e) "We can't put up our tents."

....

read

2 **Dans le dialogue page 119 de ton livre, les enfants ont raconté leur histoire dans le désordre. Recopie-la dans l'ordre en relevant uniquement ce qu'ils disent (ne recopie pas les répliques des parents).**

....

....

....

....

....

....

....

....

....

....

practise

3 **Relie les deux colonnes, puis souligne les changements entre l'énoncé direct et indirect (les énoncés 1 à 7 de la colonne 1 sont rapportés au discours indirect dans la colonne 2). Ensuite rapporte les deux dernières phrases au discours indirect.**

Discours direct	Discours indirect
1 • "He has a son", she said.	a • She wants to know where her bag is.
2 • "I'm happy", she says.	b • She says he has a son.
3 • The children: "Where is Lynn's bag?"	c • They want to know where their bag is.
4 • Lynn: "Where is my bag?"	d • She said she was happy.
5 • "I'm happy", she said.	e • She said he had a son.
6 • "He has a son", she says.	f • They want to know where her bag is.
7 • The children: "Where's our bag?"	g • She says she is happy.
8 • Lynn: "Where are the kids?"	h • ....
9 • "Scott has the painting", Gordon said.	i • ....

write

4 Voici l'interview d'un astronaute à son retour sur terre après six mois passés dans l'espace. Rapporte les questions du journaliste et les réponses de l'astronaute.

Astronaut: I'm very happy to be back on Earth!

Journalist: Tell us, what did you do all day in your space station?

Astronaut: Lots of things! I had to do a lot of sport. I had to collect things for research... I had to analyze samples*...

Journalist: What was the most difficult moment?

Astronaut: It was when my dog died of old age and I couldn't be with him...

Journalist: Now you're back on Earth, what are you going to do?

Astronaut: I'm going to go on vacation with my family!

The astronaut says he ....

The journalist wants to know ....

....

....

....

....

....

....

* samples : *échantillons*

LESSON 2

2 Listen and speak

- Le texte enregistré reproduit ici doit être caché pendant l'exercice d'écoute.
- Il te servira de modèle, au besoin, pendant l'activité orale.
- Tu pourras en mémoriser quelques phrases avant un contrôle oral ou écrit.

Dialogue A
- What is it? You look disappointed!
- I am too... We've lost the cup...four-two...
- Never mind!

Dialogue B
- Hey! What's wrong? You look furious!
- I've found this parking ticket on my car.
- Again!!

Dialogue C
Mary: Hey! What's wrong?
Her mum: A spider!
Mary: Dad! Mum's seen a spider in the living-room...

Dialogue D
- What's wrong with Karen? She looks so sad!
- It's her boyfriend...he's left her.
- Oh no, poor Karen!

Dialogue E
Jim: Hi Pam! You sound excited! What's happened?
Pam: I've passed my driving test!
Jim: Really! I can't believe it!
Pam: Oh YOU...

3 Read and understand

a) Listen and read the two letters. Can you guess the meaning of these words? (Remember "Strategies" unit 3 and 5.)

deal - guest - hope - turn out - book - rent - fetch

nouns: .... - ....

verbs: .... - .... - .... - .... - ....

b) **Choose the three sentences in the letters which correspond to the three pictures on page 121 of your book. Then, recap the main information in the two letters.**

c) **Now, look at the picture on page 123 and say all you can.**

MEMO

NEW WORDS
- mayor - deal - museum - guest
- hope - turn out - book - fetch - rent - drop - burn - score

AND NOW... THINK!

He's broken a vase.
They have scored a goal.

- **Dans ces deux phrases, souligne le groupe verbal puis complète la construction du *present perfect* :**

  - Le *present perfect* se construit avec :

  Auxiliaire : .... conjugué au .... + verbe au participe passé.

  - Le participe passé des verbes réguliers se forme en ajoutant .... à la fin du verbe. Pour les verbes irréguliers, voir liste p. 142 du livre.

- **Pourquoi appelle-t-on cette forme verbale *present perfect* ?**

  - Parce que l'auxiliaire *Have* est conjugué au ....
  - Parce que le *present perfect* permet :
    ❑ de raconter dans le détail un événement qui s'est produit dans le passé, en donnant la date, les circonstances, etc.
    ❑ de parler de la situation présente tout en évoquant un événement qui s'est produit avant, et qui a des conséquences dans le présent.

memorize

❶ **Complète ces dialogues avec les verbes suivants conjugués au *present perfect* :**
lose, find, see, leave, pass.

Dialogue A

- What is it? You look disappointed!
- I am too... We .... the cup... four-two...
- Never mind!

Dialogue B

- Hey! What's wrong? You look furious!

- I .... this parking ticket on my car.

- Again!!

Dialogue C

Mary: Hey! What's wrong?

Her mum: A spider!

Mary: Dad! Mum .... a spider in the living-room...

Dialogue D

- What's wrong with Karen? She looks so sad!

- It's her boyfriend... he .... her.

- Oh no, poor Karen!

Dialogue E

Jim: Hi Pam! You sound excited! What's happened?

Pam: I .... my driving test!

Jim: Really! I can't believe it!

Pam: Oh YOU...

read

2 Retrouve dans les deux lettres page 121 de ton livre les phrases suivantes, et note-les.

Nous avons commencé à retaper la grange.

....

Vous avez tous été merveilleux !

....

La mairie a signé le contrat.

....

J'ai réservé mon billet pour l'Angleterre.

....

practise

3 Les héros ont fini de retaper la grange et de l'équiper pour l'ouverture du club. Voici le résultat ! En utilisant les verbes fournis, dis tout ce qu'ils ont fait.

....

....

....

....

....

....

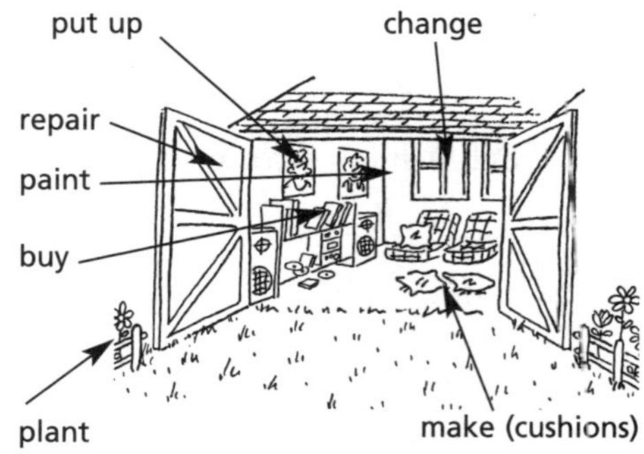

....

....

write

4 Écris la réponse de Lynn à Scott : elle va lui exprimer la joie de tous, lui parler des travaux dans la grange en lui disant ce que les enfants et M. Bailey viennent de faire, lui parler de projets pour l'été, etc. Présente ta lettre comme une vraie lettre.

RHYTHM'N SOUNDS

Dessine une flèche qui monte ou une flèche qui descend dans les espaces blancs selon que la voix monte ou descend.

We need some sugar (↗), some flour (↗), some eggs ( ) and a little milk ( ), but we don't need any chocolate. ( ) Do we need a lot of milk? ( )
No, ( ) not much, ( ) just a small cup. ( )
This book tells us the story of a dog, Buck, ( ) who learns to survive in a hostile region. ( ) It is about a company of dwarfs ( ) who search for a treasure guarded by a dragon. ( )

STRATEGIES

PART 4. POUR COMPRENDRE DANS LE DÉTAIL

B • Quel est le sujet traité dans le 4e paragraphe ? Souligne tous les mots que tu connais ou reconnais.

But life is full of danger for baby raccoons. They need to be very careful, or they will become prey to their enemies. Adult raccoons can protect themselves against many enemies. If they are attacked, they will fight very hard using their strength, intelligence and sharp teeth. But baby raccoons are not very strong and their teeth are not sharp enough! So they must be very careful!

C • Quel est le message principal de ce paragraphe ?
Relie *"they"* et *"their"* à *"baby raccoons"* ou à *"adult raccoons"*. Pour cela, souligne en rouge ce qui est à relier à *"baby raccoons"* et en bleu ce qui est à relier à *"adult raccoons"*.

....

....

D • Maintenant, tu vas deviner le sens des mots que tu ne connais pas dans cette phrase :

If they are attacked, they will fight very hard using their strength, intelligence and sharp teeth.

a) Commence par chercher leur catégorie grammaticale.

fight:	❑ verbe	❑ adjectif	❑ nom	❑ adverbe
strength:	❑ verbe	❑ adjectif	❑ nom	❑ adverbe
sharp:	❑ verbe	❑ adjectif	❑ nom	❑ adverbe

b) Utilise maintenant la logique du texte :

• **Peux-tu compléter cette phrase en français ?**

S'ils sont attaqués, ils .... en utilisant, etc.
"Fight" signifie donc : ....

• ***"Strength"* fait partie d'une énumération dans la phrase.**

Quels sont les autres mots de l'énumération ? ....
Ce sont les .... qu'utilisent les adultes pour se battre.
Dans la phrase suivante, on parle des bébés. Trouve l'adjectif qui correspond au nom *"strength"* : ....
"Strength" signifie donc : ....

• **Tu connais le mot *"teeth"* et tu sais que *"sharp"* est un adjectif.**

Trouve des adjectifs qui pourraient décrire leurs dents : ....
Lorsque les *"raccoons"* doivent se défendre, il vaut mieux que leurs dents soient .... *"Sharp"* signifie donc : ....

HIGHLIGHTS

• **Have a good look at the map and at the photos in your book page 129 and memorize the information by asking and answering questions.**
Pupil 1: How long is the Grand Canyon?
Pupil 2: It's ... long.

• **Play a memory game in groups. Close your books.**
Teacher: Name the longest canyon in the world.
Pupil 2: The Grand Canyon.
...

• **Now it's your turn! Quiz your friends.**
Team A: What's the name of the most popular soft drink in the world?
Team B: ...

LEARN YOUR WORDS

1. Associe les deux colonnes pour former des noms composés. Certains sont illustrés.

Exemple : post + office = *post office*

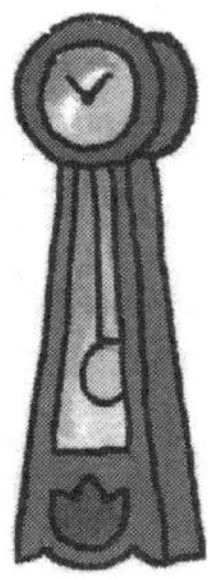

1	2
tooth	clock
girl	driver
alarm	brush
post	friend
can	opener
taxi	office
bottle	ache
bus	
grandfather	
boy	

Choisis la bonne réponse :

Dans ces noms composés, le nom principal est-il en première ❑ ou en deuxième ❑ position ?

2. Complète et recopie cette définition :

Dans un nom composé, le nom situé en …………………… position sert à préciser le nom situé en …………………… position.

3. Observe bien les exemples fournis, puis complète les tableaux. Relève les changements orthographiques et déduis-en les règles avec ton professeur.

Tableau 1

adjectif	happy	polite	sad	kind
adverbe	happily			
nom	happiness			

Tableau 2

verbe	work	watch	run	keep	paint
nom	worker				

……………………………………………………………………………………

……………………………………………………………………………………

……………………………………………………………………………………

LET'S HAVE FUN!

D'après toi, quels sont les ingrédients dont le cuisinier va avoir besoin pour préparer des *"chocolate brownies"* ? Coche-les dans la première colonne, puis vérifie en écoutant le dialogue et coche la deuxième colonne.

a) Écoute à nouveau et note les bonnes quantités.

	Your choice		Quantity : 50g, 100g, 150g, 2, half a teaspoon
1 • margarine			
2 • butter			
3 • oil			
4 • salt			
5 • eggs			
6 • caster sugar			
7 • brown sugar			
8 • milk			
9 • flour			
10 • chocolate			
11 • Mars bar			
12 • chopped peanuts			
13 • chopped walnuts			
14 • coffee flavouring			
15 • vanilla flavouring			

b) Écoute le dialogue et associe le numéro de chaque ingrédient aux verbes suivants :
Exemple : melt : *1 and 10 (margarine and chocolate).*

stir in : ....

add : ....

beat : ....

mix in : ....

c) Écris sous chaque dessin le verbe correspondant.

melt • stir in • leave to cool • add • beat • mix in • bake

....

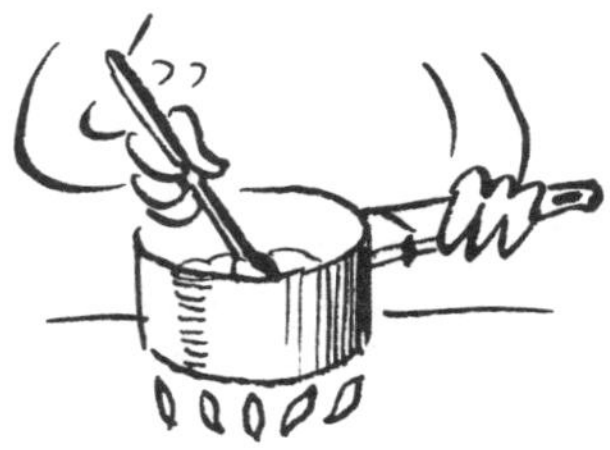
....

....

....

....

....

....

Welcome to "Radio kitchen", your favourite programme!
Betty: Good morning Luigi. And what's the recipe today?
Luigi: Good morning, Betty. Today's recipe is chocolate brownies.
Betty: Sounds delicious. So. What do we need?
Luigi: Some soft margarine and some cooking chocolate.
Betty: OK. How much margarine, first?
Luigi: A hundred grammes and fifty grammes of chocolate. You melt them together and leave them to cool.
Betty: And then, leave to cool.
Luigi: You stir in the sugar...
Betty: How much?
Luigi: 150g. Oh! I forgot, it's brown sugar.
Betty: OK, 150g of brown sugar.
Luigi: And then you add the eggs.
Betty: How many eggs do we need this time Luigi?

Luigi: 2, Betty. Beat them with some vanilla flavouring.
Betty: Do we need a lot of vanilla?
Luigi: No, not much. Half a teaspoonful. And then you mix in the flour and the walnuts.
Betty: Tell us, how much flour do we need Luigi?
Luigi: You need 100g of flour and only 50g of chopped walnuts.
Betty: Is that it?
Luigi: Don't forget to bake it Betty. Put the mixture into a buttered tin and bake for half an hour.
Betty: And then invite all your friends round for tea. Do you make a lot of cakes, Luigi?
Luigi: Every day. My children love home-made cakes!
Betty: Well, that's all for today. Tune in again tomorrow morning same time... Bye for now!

MAINTENANT TU SAIS

Lesson 1	• Parler au discours indirect	*He told us he was a ranger. Tell me who this Scott is!*
Lesson 2	• Parler du résultat dans le présent d'un événement passé	*Look! He's broken a vase! Ouch! I've burnt my finger!*
Strategies	• Avoir une attitude active pendant que tu lis en repérant le plan du texte, tout ce que tu connais ou reconnais, en te posant des questions et en devinant le sens des mots que tu ne connais pas.	
Highlights	• Comparer plusieurs choses en utilisant le superlatif.	*Coca-Cola is the best-known soft drink in the world.*

Dessins de : Ch. Quennehen, C. Proteaux et F. San Millan
Mise en pages et photogravure : AlphaStudio
Couverture : Chrystel Proupuech
Imprimerie : Hérissey à Évreux (France) - N° 101358 — Dépôt légal : Mai 2006-5053/09